T0305159

PLATFORM POLITICS

Corporate Power, Grassroots Movements
and the Sharing Economy

Luke Yates

BRISTOL
UNIVERSITY
PRESS

First published in Great Britain in 2025 by

Bristol University Press
University of Bristol
1–9 Old Park Hill
Bristol
BS2 8BB
UK
t: +44 (0)117 374 6645
e: bup-info@bristol.ac.uk

Details of international sales and distribution partners are available at bristoluniversitypress.co.uk

© Bristol University Press 2025

British Library Cataloguing in Publication Data
A catalogue record for this book is available from the British Library

ISBN 978-1-5292-3614-9 hardcover
ISBN 978-1-5292-3615-6 paperback
ISBN 978-1-5292-3616-3 ePub
ISBN 978-1-5292-3617-0 ePdf

The right of Luke Yates to be identified as author of this work has been asserted by him in accordance with the Copyright, Designs and Patents Act 1988.

All rights reserved: no part of this publication may be reproduced, stored in a retrieval system, or transmitted in any form or by any means, electronic, mechanical, photocopying, recording, or otherwise without the prior permission of Bristol University Press.

Every reasonable effort has been made to obtain permission to reproduce copyrighted material. If, however, anyone knows of an oversight, please contact the publisher.

The statements and opinions contained within this publication are solely those of the author and not of the University of Bristol or Bristol University Press. The University of Bristol and Bristol University Press disclaim responsibility for any injury to persons or property resulting from any material published in this publication.

Bristol University Press works to counter discrimination on grounds of gender, race, disability, age and sexuality.

Cover design: Andrew Corbett
Front cover image: Alamy/jory mundy
Bristol University Press uses environmentally responsible print partners.
Printed and bound in Great Britain by CPI Group (UK) Ltd, Croydon, CR0 4YY

FSC
www.fsc.org
MIX
Paper | Supporting
responsible forestry
FSC® C013604

Contents

Acknowledgements

Thanks to my interviewees, who made this book possible. Many thanks also to Alan Warde, Andy McMeekin and Sam Hind for reading earlier versions of this work; to Tim Hunt and Rob Harrison at Ethical Consumer; to the four anonymous reviewers of the book proposal and the two anonymous readers of the manuscript; and to my editors Paul Stevens and Ellen Mitchell. All errors are my own.

1

Introducing Platform Politics

This is a story about the power of grassroots movements, narratives and modern corporations to change the way everyday life is provisioned and governed. From 2008, a new wave of Silicon Valley corporations refined a 'platform' business model, providing digitally mediated versions of a number of existing services. Several companies, including Airbnb and Uber, and a host of allies, advocates and alternative economic projects, created a story about a new economy with 'sharing' and 'collaboration' at its centre. These *lean platforms*, holding few assets but playing a coordinating role between workers, owners and consumers, started to be presented as an answer to the problems of contemporary neoliberal economies.

Yet it has become widely recognised that the predicted benefits of the platform economy are not materialising. This book charts the rise and fall of the morally laden narratives generated early on in terms such as the 'Collaborative' or 'Sharing Economy', identifying the popular stories told about platforms and the dynamics of change associated with them. It explores the growing context of growing resistance to platforms and attempts to transform or regulate them, and it analyses and theorises the tactics platform businesses use to try to consolidate their advantages.

In doing so, the book works with a unique set of interviews with ex-workers of the lean platform business Airbnb, who were responsible for designing and implementing platform political strategies, particularly around the political mobilisation of platform users and allies, *platform power*. The book brings in a supplementary body of statements and documents which demonstrate how platform political tactics work in practice. The book also makes use of such public documents and statements such as those of Airbnb's former Head of Global Community, Douglas Atkin, who in his role spearheaded the company's political strategy to avoid regulation: the mass mobilisation of thousands of landlords since 2010, deploying 'Community Organisers' trained in electoral campaigning, non-governmental organisations and charities. An excerpt from a speech by

Atkin characterises the combination of rhetorical and mobilisation tactics at the centre of platform politics:

> And this is our problem at the moment. Airbnb and many other sharing economy companies. The sharing economy or peer economy is new, but the laws are old. And we're bumping up against old laws and old incumbents, many of whom have had long deep pockets and a long-term relationships with governments. That's why Brian Chesky, the CEO, one of the founders of Airbnb, asked me to figure out how to mobilise the community because we're using people now as a way of demonstrating that this is a good thing for cities and a good thing for citizens. ... Basically, we drenched lawmakers with our community. (Atkin 2014)

Examining these interviews and public facing materials reveals practices at the cutting edge of lobbying and corporate campaigning. Platform businesses borrow heavily from the repertoires of civil society, social movements, and electoral politics, and have hired hundreds of professionals from these worlds to establish campaigns, while misleadingly presenting the resultant grassroots initiatives as independent of the companies. Platform politics is controversial and contested, even, the findings show, by those directly implementing it.

The book builds on and is inspired by a growing body of literature on platform regulation and tech imaginaries; platform tactics around user mobilisation and rhetoric; critical journalism; and wider debates around civil society, neoliberalism and technology. It is the first book-length study of the political struggles and movements shaping digital platforms. It analyses the conflicts around more than one platform business, allowing for a review of the tactics of platforms across several sectors. The book provides in-depth analysis of *platform power*, a phenomenon referring to lobbying innovations in which businesses are able to mobilise their users and allies against regulation through the exploitation of customer data. Based on the empirical data gathered, combined with a review of existing sources, the book presents a new framework for analysing platform power: a typology of four distinct modes of mobilising users and allies, and a summary of the five ways that platform power differs from existing forms of corporate political activity. The findings and theoretical developments throw light on the way that platform economy businesses have developed and innovated around existing forms of corporate power, political activity and lobbying and entrenching governance challenges associated with neoliberalism. In mainstreaming corporate civic initiatives, platform businesses challenge traditional ideas about social movements and civil society safeguarding and enhancing democracy.

The scope of these arguments is specific. The term *platform* is now very widely used to refer to digital service providers such as Google, Amazon, Facebook, Apple and Microsoft, and to dynamics of the 'digital economy' that are becoming the foundations for organising services and exchanges across society (Van Dijck et al 2018). Especially, though, the term has been used to describe a group of businesses sometimes known as *lean platforms* (Srnicek 2016) and most often associated with the concept of the platform economy. These businesses are the focus of this book. They include Airbnb, Uber, Deliveroo, Amazon Mechanical Turk, DiDi, Instacart, Doordash, Meituan, HackerRank, OnlyFans, and many others. Lean platforms are understood, following Srnicek (2016), as digital intermediary businesses which play a role in connecting and matching producers and consumers, the businesses themselves holding few or no assets.

Lean platforms, like many other technology companies, exhibit a political economic model where venture capital is used to grow rapidly, initially disregarding returns on investment, destroying existing industries and competitors, and achieving network effects where increased size and scale improves the service, further squeezing out competitors, achieving monopoly status and, potentially, complete market dominance. Their strategy of swift growth at almost any cost means that the existence of platforms is predicated on ignoring or changing the law to protect their regulatory advantages vis-à-vis competitors (Pollman and Barry 2016). This means that the core business models of lean platforms are normally either initially illegal or appear to operate in a legal grey area. This, alongside effects on workers and housing, as well as taxation and competition, creates acrimony. The conflicts reveal competing visions for the economy, governance and even democracy. Many of the processes described using data and examples from lean platforms, however, have some parallels in findings around other digital platform businesses, and even non-platform businesses. They include elements of platform rhetoric that are described in Chapter 2, and some of the dynamics of regulatory struggle that are summarised in Chapter 3. Some of the political tactics of lean platforms have also inspired practices elsewhere, a finding discussed in Chapters 4 and 6.

Platform Politics is particularly interested in understanding change and explanations of change. In the worlds of transportation, accommodation, food delivery, employment and other areas of social life, platforms have been linked to fundamental transformations. They concern the way that goods and services are created, distributed and consumed. Understanding these socioeconomic changes is widely understood as an urgent task for social science. The book interrogates how platform businesses contribute to policy changes, and the wider trends they emerge from and are contributing towards.

The theme is important because of a fundamental analytical bias in mainstream accounts of digital transformation by both advocates and critics, popular and academic, in regularly presenting platform businesses as the only actor with any real power in the story of digital transformation, generating changes around home, work and property. States, social movements, other corporations and populations are framed as bystanders, or inert in a process of inevitable modernisation. This narrative, whether Uber, Airbnb, Deliveroo and others are cast as heroes or villains, obscures the actual processes underpinning change. It skates over the dramatically different outcomes that have already emerged across the societies where the businesses operate. The simplification also inhibits the analysis of potential alternative future trajectories of technological development, those that might better reflect the needs of users, workers and societies.

This book, in contrast to this dominant narrative, argues that protests, boycotts, state support or opposition, referendums, strikes, lobbying, acrimony and argument have been fundamental to the transformation associated with platform capitalism. The struggles shape how platform businesses are understood, and the way they unfold in a society. They also affect political norms themselves, changing the ways in which corporations, states and civil society engage with each other, and posing new, contentious interpretations of governance and democracy. The book, as the title suggests, focuses particularly on the contradictory ways in which grassroots movements play a part in contesting and advancing corporate power and the idea of the Sharing Economy: in advocating visions of technological progress; in contesting the impacts of platform businesses; and – where the book makes its main contribution – in defending businesses from state regulation or other disruptive change.

What forms does platform politics take?

In response to conflicts and attempts to regulate the sector, platform businesses have developed a repertoire of political tactics for engaging with states and societies. The circumstances and contexts in which platform businesses exercise these tactics are necessary to understand their nature. Differentiating the term platform politics here (although overlaps mean that the book discusses more than one facet of platform politics at any one time) helps in characterising these processes.

- Platform politics includes the discursive framing of the platform economy, or so-called Sharing Economy, and its effects: *platform rhetoric*. Contentious categories such as the Sharing or Collaborative Economy bundle together Silicon Valley corporations with initiatives like Freecycle, the sharing of drills, and social movements such as Ouishare. Platform rhetoric involved lobbying by companies and boosterism by consultants which secured significant early institutional support for an entire wave of businesses and practices. Thus, the collaborative economy, the European Commission declared in 2016, held 'significant potential to contribute to competitiveness and growth ... to promote new employment opportunities, flexible working arrangements and new sources of income' (European Commission 2016). Platform rhetoric includes some subtle but important epistemological claims. It redefines business users as a community or movement; platforms as democracy; states as monopolies; regulation as quaint and outdated; and it presents a narrative of technological determinism where any form of resistance, civic or state-coordinated, is fought against the rising tide of inevitable technological progress. The book builds on important detailed existing work on platform rhetoric (Slee 2015, Martin 2016, Murillo et al 2017, Mikołajewska-Zajac 2019, Rosenblat 2019, Van Doorn 2020, Del Nido 2021, Schüßlr et al 2021). Platform rhetoric is discussed throughout the book, but especially in Chapters 2 and 3, and how it works together with other tactics in Chapters 3, 4 and 5. It intimately concerns the question of *what the platform economy is*, still something of an open question, and the implications of this uncertainty for being able to govern and change it.

- Platform politics also concerns the disenchantment with and defiance of this story: *platform dissent*. Recently, platform dissent has become increasingly studied. It takes place in campaigns, protests and union recruitment drives, from anti-gentrification movements, to strikes, to alliances of city mayors, and a host of data activists and critical commentators (see, for example, Cant 2019, Novy and Colomb 2019, Boewe and Schulten 2020, Nieuwland and van Melik 2020, Woodcock 2021, Wood and Lehdonvirta 2021, Stabrowski 2022, Wilson et al 2022, Cini 2023, Colomb and Moreira de Souza 2023, Fernández-Trujillo et al 2023, Soriano 2023, Vrikki and Lekakis 2023). These actors and projects have challenged the Sharing Economy narrative and questioned its tropes of technological determinism, inevitable creative destruction, or 'disruption'. Dissenters are founding alternative visions and initiatives and are fighting for housing and employment rights, with increasing success. Through accounts, often by workers themselves, we can see that lean platforms are facing the biggest challenges yet to their economic and political dominance, even while the biggest continue to grow. Platform dissent, the challenge that it represents to the platforms, and the accompanying political struggles, has dramatically changed narratives around the new digital economy in the last ten years, and has recently led to enforceable regulation to protect housing and employment rights. It is at the basis of not only the possibility of regulation, but possible futures in which the control and ownership of digital platforms is held by societies, users and workers themselves. While existing literature reviews the forms that platform dissent has taken directly, this book focuses on the contexts and drivers of the dissent, in Chapter 2, the trajectories taken by the conflicts, in Chapter 3, and the tactics of platform businesses to neutralise it in Chapters 4 and 5.

• Platform politics, most importantly for this book, also refers to the reaction by platform businesses to this dissent, the tactics developed in attempts to maintain and consolidate their positions and political and economic advantages: *platform power* (Lynskey 2017, Culpepper and Thelen 2020). Platform power builds and complements intensive and high-level private lobbying by lean platforms such as those exposed in the Uber Files leak of 2022, with even more controversial tactics for lobbying politicians and the public: the mass mobilising of users and allies and their misleading presentation as independent political activists in the face of regulation. This has taken the form of scores of petitions set up by businesses themselves to 'save' them; corporate-sponsored protests; coordinated and rehearsed responses to public consultations; and new civil society groups such as Airbnb's 'Host Clubs' – seemingly independent grassroots groups which advocate on behalf of the platform's preferred legislation. The book reviews and builds on the growing literature discussing platform power (Pollman and Barry 2016, Collier et al 2018, Thelen 2018, Culpepper and Thelen 2020, Van Doorn 2020, Stabrowski 2022, Lehdonvirta 2022). The tactics, understood as partial innovations to the practices of 'corporate grassroots lobbying', work alongside platform rhetoric, the claims to legitimacy by platform businesses. Platform power is discussed in Chapters 3, 4 and 5.

• Finally, the book is concerned with the imaginaries, potential and future of the new digital economy: *platform possibility*. Platform possibility reflects the attempted imposition of a particular possible future by platform businesses – one in which their technologies seamlessly and inevitably transform reality. It also reflects the very real contingency of the political economic landscape, even in circumstances where power is unevenly distributed. There are significant differences across what different businesses, policy makers, users, workers and tenants want the future to look like, underpinning the struggles among them. In this way, we can imagine very different arrangements and forms of governance around digital platforms (for example, Frase 2016, Bastani 2019, Lehdonvirta 2022, Muldoon 2022, Varoufakis 2023). Whose vision prevails is subject to tensions, competition and contradictions among elites, regulation, popular dissent, debate, resistance and other forms of political struggle. Ideas about and struggles over futures run through the book but are discussed in most depth in Chapters 2 and 6.

To what extent does platform politics vary across businesses, contexts and time periods? How different were the politics of platforms in 2010 to the struggles of 2024? What do struggles around food delivery have in common with those around short-term accommodation? Are there differences between businesses in the same sector, with 'good' and 'bad' players? What variation and similarities are there across contexts and sectors in the use of defensive strategies such as platform power? How are the narratives and tactics of platforms deployed in different contexts, and how does understanding the detail of these practices help in explaining their different outcomes? And what lessons are there for understanding even newer tech platforms and services, and the contemporary nature of corporate power and democratic governance? These are the questions that recent work, at last beginning to treat change as contingent and as the outcome of struggles and negotiations, has begun to address, and towards which this book contributes (for example, Collier et al 2018, Thelen 2018, Chan and Kwok 2021, Colomb and Moreira de Souza 2021, Aguilera et al 2025).

The book, therefore, adds to the recent and growing work examining political interactions around platform businesses. It contributes to understandings of the platform economy and the changes it is part of by identifying, contextualising, investigating and theorising the core tactics of platform businesses, widely regarded as pivotal to platform politics, and the dynamics of the interactions between platform businesses, their contexts and their opponents. In doing so, the book also identifies concepts and themes for thinking about platform politics that speak to current debates among scholars, activists and policy makers.

How can we understand platform politics?

How can we understand, theorise and empirically explore platform politics? One answer is that its levers, language and its outcomes are all around us. It is visible in ubiquitous posters, stickers and graffiti (see Figure 1.1) in the most popular tourist destinations of the 21st century, where movements and governments in Amsterdam, Athens, Lisbon, Venice, Paris and Barcelona have led calls for changes in tourism policy around holiday flats due to the scale of long-term housing lost to Airbnb and Booking.com (Novy and Colomb 2019, Aguilera et al 2025). It is palpable in the remarkable and new linguistic flexibility in ways of using words like 'sharing', 'trust' and 'democracy' in many platform companies' public relations (PR) materials and sympathetic commentary. It is asserted in their disaster relief initiatives and Black Lives Matter support statements. And it is obvious in the strikes, the layoffs and the whistleblowers that have repeatedly made the headlines in recent years. The ubiquity of platform politics, indeed, raises the question of where it starts and ends. Boundaries around platforms are notoriously

Figure 1.1: Anti-Airbnb stickers and graffiti in Madrid, Thessaloniki and Steamboat Springs, Colorado

Source: Images from Radical Graffiti

difficult to draw, some influentially suggesting that we begin to think of platforms as a paradigm, a singular noun, or verb, as a mode of organising (for example, Helmond 2015, Bratton 2016, Nieborg and Poell 2018). While the lean platforms I cover in *Platform Politics* are a subset of a particular sort, and my claims relate primarily to them, there are visible political dynamics across the media platforms like Facebook/Meta, X, Google, Microsoft, Apple and Amazon, from Australia and Spain challenging Google and Facebook/Meta's hold over media advertising revenue, to India rejecting Facebook/Meta's plan to provide and restrict internet access in its Internet.org/Free Basics project, to the multiple anti-trust cases against Google. New apps making use of artificial intelligence large language models, meanwhile, suggest a further wave of transformation in the way that information and data are accessed and gathered, with further implications for employment, education and art; and creating additional challenges for governance and democracy.

Much is in plain sight. And the use of some platform political approaches, especially platform rhetoric, and the exercise of platform power, deploying users and allies as advocates of the brand, brings political disputes and influence, in some ways, directly into apparently open public debate. Despite evidence of platform businesses engaging in typical lobbying, including secret and undocumented meetings with politicians, this citizen lobbying appears to shift the interface of corporate political activity into public debate and forums. Indeed, we also know an enormous amount simply by drawing together accounts of existing struggles, statements from chief executive officers and other spokespeople or advisors, scraping websites and monitoring records, as much literature in the area has profitably explored (see, for example, Morozov 2013, Van Doorn 2020, Muldoon 2022). Do these rich sources of data represent a new ethos of corporate transparency and a commitment to accountability by platform businesses?

No. The information, speeches, press releases, platform-commissioned research, innovative PR materials and other platform-derived documentation, it has become obvious, are as disingenuous as they are copious. In many cases, when attempting to gather data or information about actual processes or solid statistics about the political activities of lean platform businesses, their representatives have been obstructive and evasive. Platform rhetoric, the language of Uber, Deliveroo and other platforms, has been so misleading that their efforts to redefine employment relationships, wages, recruitment, sharing and hospitality are repeatedly described by journalists and activists as 'doublespeak' or 'newspeak', a deliberately obtuse approach to communication itself that captures the authoritarian potential of repurposing language as imagined in George Orwell's classic dystopia *1984*. For platform workers on employment contracts, and even for short-term contracts, non-disclosure agreements and non-disparagement clauses are commonplace. The case of the Uber leaks in summer 2022 demonstrated that platform businesses have not shifted their approach to lobbying, but have simply diversified it, in some cases appearing to endanger drivers' lives in the process. Uber's 'Greyball' and 'kill switch' technologies were used to obscure and destroy any possible access to transparency or legal accountability when raided by law enforcement (Davies et al 2022). Airbnb hides the identities of hosts and locations of illegal listings, routinely refuses to remove illegal listings, routinely refuses to provide data for enforcement of local laws, and when permits are mandatory and the levels of illegal listings have been publicly revealed, it has simply removed the permit number section from listings in this area (Cox and Haar 2020). Airbnb is reported to have paid millions of dollars in settlement payouts to avoid public knowledge of the accidents and problems faced by those using the platform (Carville 2021). Lean platforms also inhibit the enforcement of regulations through evasion tactics that are reviewed in Chapter 3.

In researching the politics of digital platforms, the data needed to appreciate what is happening or to hold platforms democratically accountable is usually missing or withheld. Power relations which make platforms difficult to regulate are not only reproduced, but are constituted, by the massive advantages held by platforms reluctant to share their data (Zuboff 2019). To analyse platforms and platform politics, it is necessary to distinguish and interrogate these approaches to information, rhetoric, data and knowledge, and assess their impacts.

This means that empirical evidence and analysis from scholars and journalists are in great demand if we want to understand the practices of platform politics. This book therefore presents a combination of these data that are widely available, a collection of secondary sources and documents relating to platform struggles since 2008, supplementing a dataset of much more specific empirical contributions, that help uncover some of the relationships and processes which underpin platform politics in terms of platforms' own political tactics, the particular and allegedly new approach to corporate political action that has been called, as I do here, 'platform power' (Culpepper and Thelen 2020), as well as 'regulatory entrepreneurship' (Pollman and Barry 2016, Van Doorn 2020) and 'corporate populism' (Nyberg and Murray 2023), among other terms.

I draw especially on a unique case study of rich data around the political tactics of Airbnb, home to the most intensive and sustained platform-sponsored grassroots lobbying strategy in the world so far, through interviews with former Airbnb public policy staff working across 14 national contexts. These staff reveal a rapidly changing world of corporate power, and a sense of unease even from those most intimately involved in delivering it. The case study charts the rise of these PR, lobbying and civil society practices into and through the platform economy, and their influences far beyond it.[1]

Organisation of chapters and how to read this book

Platform Politics speaks to public debates about the nature and implications of digital transformation and tech power in relation to, work, housing and consumption. It may also be of relevance to activists, policy makers, journalists, platform workers and users, and those most directly affected by platforms. It is, at the same time, a book by an academic, intended to enhance understandings of the new digital economy, corporate political activity, power, civil society and social movements, and urban processes, and so will be of interest to researchers and students in various areas, including sociology, human geography, urban studies, anthropology, political science, science and technology studies, law, and business studies. Each chapter stands alone, making it possible to dip into single chapters if necessary without too much confusion.

Chapter 2 is entitled 'Contested Stories of Platform Capitalism: Crisis, Legitimacy and Platform Rhetoric'. Its main argument is that the ways that we understand platforms, what they are, where they come from and where they are going, performatively shape the future. The emphasis is on platform rhetoric, the stories, categories and semantic games around lean platforms used in avoiding calls for their regulation or subjection to other forms of democratic ownership or control. It describes the emergence of lean platforms in the context of the 2008 economic crisis, and their contradictory relationship with neoliberalism: being dependent on many elements of this context, and politically requiring deregulation, yet presenting themselves as addressing the problems of the crisis and of neoliberalism. This leads into a discussion which maps the rise and fall of the morally laden notion of the Sharing Economy, a term which has long generated confusion. The chapter discusses narratives around change and the future, where platforms are often presented as modernity and progress; important in denying the legitimacy of state regulation, and asserting the futility of resisting platform business aims. Finally, the language used by lean platforms, their 'phrasebook', is analysed, focusing in particular on the ways that work, platform corporations themselves, and democracy, are redefined.

Chapter 3 is entitled 'Trajectories of Struggle around Lean Platforms: Making Sense of Change'. It reviews and analyses what happens in conflicts around platforms, identifying common processes and tactical approaches. The trajectories are characterised, in the argument, in three sets of processes, with distinctive platform tactics employed in each. The first, *incursion, expansion and habituation*, describes and discusses the tactic of arriving in a jurisdiction without asking permission or notifying authorities and ignoring extant legislation, and rapidly expanding, developing relationships with users which can subsequently be exploited in the case of regulatory challenge. This sets the groundwork for the process of *politicisation, framing and mobilisation*, where a platform is challenged, a process of questioning or politicising issues, by social movements, unions or state institutions. This is met with the processes widely seen as most significant, and most innovative, of platforms in the context of struggles: confrontational platform rhetoric and the mobilisation of users and allies in platform power. It is the two processes of framing and corporate mobilisation which are examined in the previous and subsequent chapters. Finally, there are frequently ongoing challenges around *inhibiting enforcement*, through tactics of *non-cooperation*, *withholding data, stalling and venue-shifting* which aim to prevent, delay or overturn unwanted regulations.

Chapters 4 and 5 build on this analysis by investigating the dynamics of how platforms' mobilisation and narrative framing approaches (platform power and rhetoric) intersect and overlap in practice. While the extant literature depicts a huge range of forms of mobilisation, Chapter 4, 'The Practices of Platform Power: A Typology', identifies four main approaches to platform power used by platform businesses, each of which has influences from other sectors, most prominently tobacco, pharmaceutical and fossil fuel industries, and from other contexts. These approaches are, the *temporary mobilisation* of platform users and allies in short-term initiatives to oppose or neutralise political threats, the selecting and editing of the personal 'stories' of user-lobbyists in *curated storytelling* where individual testimonies become the basis of narrative frames used in public consultations and media exercises; the creation of *front groups*, allowing businesses to construct third-party entities to engage in civil society and with policy makers on their behalf; and *grassroots alliances*, where grassroots partners are identified and mobilised in exchange for donations or in-kind services; all ways of building legitimacy and placing pressure on policy makers through practices and discursive frames adapted from civil society. These underline the arguments of other analyses of platform power, including Pollman and Barry (2016), Culpepper and Thelen (2020) and others, but add several elements to their perspectives. Each approach to mobilisation is illustrated with examples from the literature and from the case study of Airbnb. The chapter also identifies the five ways in which platform power is distinctive from existing corporate grassroots lobbying, arguing that platforms build on and innovate around existing lobbying practices. It finishes by locating platform power in a wider set of trends around neoliberalism and corporate influence.

Chapter 5, 'Manufacturing a Movement: Platform Power at Airbnb', zooms in on Airbnb's platform power initiatives, exploring the processes by which, and the extent to which, a social movement or civil society initiative can be created by a platform business, using the most well-resourced example of platform-based corporate grassroots lobbying in the world to date, Airbnb Citizen. It has two main sections. First it discusses the creation of the Airbnb Citizen – the core way in which Airbnb displaces itself by claiming to represent a community – by asking the question of how prospective landlord activists are selected, and the processes through which they are subsequently recruited, trained and mobilised. It finds that participation in Airbnb's political campaigns and the composition of Home Sharing Clubs is carefully curated, with commercial landlords on the platform, the most controversial and accounting for a majority of listings, excluded, apparently in order to present a more benign narrative of the company. Interviewees describe an extensive search for appropriate recruits, followed by an intensive series of meetings and meet-ups with those who have 'good stories', building trust and gradually building up their 'asks' of recruits, which become increasingly political and involve greater responsibility. Specific landlords' personal biographies or curated 'stories' are collected and subsequently used in marketing frames, press conferences, media, and for court hearings and campaigns to lobby key decision makers. The chapter also identifies the forms of support and influence that Airbnb offers landlord activists. These include the political or civic education of landlords, the identification of political opportunities, the selecting and curating of selected user stories, the editing of these stories, preparation and rehearsal with public policy or PR staff, the creation of placards, co-participation in protests, chartering buses to transport activists to hearings, and suggesting preferred political goals and policy that landlords fight for.

The final chapter reprises the key arguments of the book and reflects on the implications of its findings for debates around corporate power, political activity and lobbying in the context of innovation; social movements and civil society; and the new digital economy. It finishes by reflecting, finally, on the alternative ways that platforms and platform commentators have imagined the future. It discusses the increasing number of imaginaries and scenarios circulating in this space, and the ways in which arguments about contingency, critique and political struggle are beginning to displace and debunk prevailing narratives of technological determinism.

2

Contested Stories of Platform Capitalism: Crisis, Legitimacy and Platform Rhetoric

The Sharing Economy reflects the crisis

While debates about the politics of digital platforms are crucial for employment rights and housing, they also concern legitimacy, corporate power and contemporary capitalism. That is because of the context for the emergence of lean platforms, their claims about their relationship to the global financial crisis, and the difficulties in their regulation and governance so far. This chapter is about the *context* to the emergence of lean platforms, and *platform rhetoric*, the constellation of stories, categories and semantic games used by platforms and their allies to frame and shape reality in a way intended to shape regulation through processes and trajectories that are described in Chapters 3, 4 and 5.

Since the 2007/2008 crisis, and arguably since the alter-globalisation movement, economic orthodoxies and common sense around neoliberalism have become increasingly scrutinised and challenged. The financial crash and its main drivers, especially the sub-prime mortgage boom in the United States, is widely regarded to have resulted from the quintessentially neoliberal deregulation of banking sectors, especially the 1999 repeal of elements of the US Glass-Steagal Act, which once again permitted financial institutions to engage in banking alongside riskier investment operations (Krugman 2008, Stiglitz 2010, Aalbers 2016). The subsequent bailouts of banks at the expense of populations, through public service austerity, and the recessions that followed, led to wage stagnation, underemployment, price rises and a global wave of outrage around the compromising of democracy, peaking between 2010 and 2013 in the so-called 'Arab Spring' and the Occupy movements (Brannen et al 2020, Bevins 2023).

The rise of new digital platforms was made possible by the neoliberal response to a crisis of neoliberal capitalism. At the same time, platforms presented themselves as part of the answer. Platforms, it was argued, were part of an alternative economic model that opposed incumbent corporate elites with a collaborative and communitarian alternative (see the section on 'The rise and fall of the Sharing Economy category').

Several wider transformations of capitalism and digital technology are helpful in contextualising the emergence, significance and power of platform businesses. Nick Srnicek (2016) notes the long-term decline in economic growth since the 1970s, the shift towards a new growth model in the West based on low interest rates, low spending, low mortgage rates and housing bubbles, the increase in long-term unemployment or underemployment and increasingly flexible labour forces, the emergence of a 'growth before profits' model in the 1990s, the recent 'hoarding' of reserves especially by technology companies, and a huge wave of investment in risky services and investment opportunities, the latest in platforms themselves. Srnicek is especially interested in the technology companies that have preceded and accompanied the emergence of lean platforms such as Uber, Airbnb, Deliveroo and others, especially Google, Facebook/Meta, Microsoft, Apple, Siemens and General Electric, which have earlier origins but have also grown rapidly since the crisis. Srnicek also notes that several characteristics of platform businesses augment their economic power, including their systemic and strategic importance in computing and logistics infrastructure for shaping and supporting institutions, states and everyday practices (Bratton 2016), their dynamism in terms of apparent innovation, and the close relationship they have had with their users. These factors, Srnicek argues, have brought about a new and hegemonic common sense (see also Slee 2015), in which 'cities are to become smart, businesses must be disruptive, workers are to become flexible, and governments must be lean and intelligent' (Srnicek 2016: 5). The accumulating resources of tech companies thus translates into both growing power vis-à-vis all companies and institutions (Van Dijck et al 2018, Lehdonvirta 2022), while also influentially defining societal problems and solutions, and in embodying tropes of innovation, dynamism, entrepreneurialism and disruption (Morozov 2013). This common sense can be seen as a reformulation and revindication of the meaning and value of neoliberal capitalism even in the context of a crisis of neoliberal capitalism. Platform businesses capture and crystallise recent economic history, and they embody a political economic orthodoxy, meaning that to study platform politics is to study the contemporary state of neoliberalism, its tensions, its structure and its ideology.

The term *platform* is now very widely used to refer to digital service providers and to dynamics of the digital economy that are becoming foundational for organising services and exchanges (Van Dijck et al 2018). My argument, as described in the introduction, focuses on a smaller group of businesses sometimes also known as *lean platforms* (Srnicek 2016). These digital intermediary businesses normally play a role in connecting and matching producers and consumers, the businesses themselves holding few or no assets. It is also these businesses that are most often associated with the *platform economy*, the focus of this book's analysis. They include Airbnb, Uber, Deliveroo, Amazon Mechanical Turk, DiDi, Instacart, Coinbase, Doordash, Meituan, HackerRank, OnlyFans, and many others. Lean platforms, and some other technology companies which offer different services and may own significant assets, also make use of a political economic model distinctive among Silicon Valley companies, where venture capital is used to grow very rapidly, initially disregarding returns on investment, destroying existing industries and competitors and achieving network effects (where size and scale improves the service, further squeezing out competitors), achieving monopoly status and market dominance (Srnicek 2016, Hoffman and Yeh 2018, Muldoon 2022, Varoufakis 2023).

The rise and fall of the Sharing Economy category

While lean platforms benefited from the crisis, in terms of being powered by a wave of even cheaper credit and labour, newly precarious home-owners, and public transportation cutbacks; many of their stories have explicitly referenced the crisis in justifying their actions. Lean platform businesses incorporated an anti-corporate critique, positioning themselves against, and promising to disrupt, an incumbent economic elite of businesses who were blamed for stifling innovation and growth. For example, Airbnb regularly rhetorically contrasted the interests and power of its 'community' with the hotel lobby and the hotel industry, while Uber regularly criticised what it called 'the Big Taxi cartel'. Platform businesses and other tech giants were plucky, anti-establishment outsiders. In the period of their rapid expansion they seemed to provide answers to the economic challenges of the period.

The concept of the Sharing or Collaborative Economy, terms formulated by consultants and investors, championed by banks and think-tanks, and popularised in management literature and the media, thus co-opted the growing interest, since the crisis, in alternative economic arrangements. It suggested that lean platforms, community tool libraries, cooperatives, and niche non-profit or even anti-capitalist projects, were all part of the same new sector (Botsman and Rogers 2010, Sundararajan 2016). Neighbourhoods were facing down economic risks by pooling their resources and engaging in forms of mutual aid and economic alternatives such as food coops (Conill et al 2012); this was presented as the same essential process as workers subsidising their reduced wages with occasional gig work, or residents weathering the growing housing crisis by renting a spare room (Botsman and Rogers 2010, Sundararajan 2016). This section, and the next, discuss the trajectory of the idea of the Sharing Economy, and the story it tells about the future, respectively, before zooming out to a wider set of rhetorical stories made by the businesses around redefining work, business and democracy.

The Collaborative and Sharing Economy,[1] which I generally refer to in short-hand as the Sharing Economy, carried several constellations of promises. These promises were about prosperity, resilience, inclusivity and conviviality, the sector theoretically encouraging ways in which more and more people would flourish as entrepreneurs, while sharing and collaboration would strengthen community and social capital (Mikołajewska-Zając 2019). Through reducing the production of new drills and cars, which would be shared more widely, and by reducing the economies of scale associated with normal ownership (Bardhi and Eckhardt 2012, Yates 2018), the Sharing Economy might shift society's orientation towards goods and services from owning them to accessing them. This reduction in ownership, in turn, would have two benefits. It would move society away from materialism, a widely held anxiety about the moral consequences of a society dominated by consumption (for example, Wilk 2001, Marcuse 2002 [1964], Schor 2007). It would also help move societies towards sustainable consumption. In the words of Botsman and Rogers (2010: xvi), collaborative consumption would 'provide significant environmental benefits by increasing use efficiency, reducing waste, encouraging the development of better products, and mopping up the surplus created by over-production and -consumption'. The Sharing Economy would even improve the rights of workers, and – as we will discuss in the final section of the chapter – enhance democracy (Mathews 2014).

Job advertisements for lean platforms, especially those in public policy, are explicit about the idea of the Sharing Economy being a fundamental element of the *political* argument for platform companies' societal benefits and their deregulation. An excerpt from a typical job advertisement in Airbnb's public policy team from May 2022 illustrates this: 'Airbnb's public policy team exists to further the interests of our community of hosts and guests with politicians, regulators, opinion leaders and others who shape the political and legal context for our business, helping them to understand the significant social and economic contributions of "the sharing economy"' (Airbnb Careers 2022).[2]

Such platform rhetoric, applied both publicly and in private lobbying, helped the platform businesses which were part of the sector rapidly secure institutional support from many governments and institutions for the remarkable potential societal benefits that would arise from the further growth of the Sharing Economy conflation. By 2016 the European Commission announced that the collaborative economy held 'significant potential to contribute to competitiveness and growth ... to promote new employment opportunities, flexible working arrangements and new sources of income' (European Commission 2016: 2). The Chinese government's 13th Five Year Plan for 2016–2020, similarly, sought to 'ensure the formation of a new pattern of internet-based collaboration and division of work ... and develop the sharing economy' (PRC 2015: 73–74). Valuations of the Sharing Economy primarily evaluated the revenues of short-term lettings, ride-hailing and delivery platforms. A variety of profit and non-profit initiatives, some tiny and used by a few hundred people, some already valued at tens of billions of US dollars, were therefore included. This important synthesis, contained in the term Sharing Economy, and the composite nature of the category, effectively hypothesised a significant future expansion in the communitarian 'sharing' of goods that are rarely used or used inefficiently, through investment into companies who called themselves sharing or collaborative. The community, reciprocity, hospitality, thrift and trust that is visible in non-profit initiatives and some more benign start-ups such as Couchsurfing thus might be 'scaled up' (Slee 2015: 15) by the businesses. Institutional support and approval for the idea of the Sharing or Collaborative Economy shaped the early years of platform regulation and debate.

A more balanced appreciation of the impacts of lean platform businesses began to enter mainstream debates from around 2014, which gradually began to manifest in critiques of the category itself. Important data emerged capturing the problems associated with the intensification of precarious work without employment rights that was characteristic of the ride-hailing and meal delivery platforms (for example, Rosenblat and Stark 2016, Scholz 2017). Analysis of the relationship between increasing numbers of short-term lets and the housing crisis suggests that short-term lettings drive up rents and contribute to the displacement of local residents (Arias-Sans and Quaglieri 2016, Cócola-Gant 2016, Wachsmuth and Weisler 2018, Cócola-Gant and Gago 2021). Exploration of the working conditions of meal delivery workers and Uber drivers showed workers struggling to subsist on fluctuating and sometimes diminishing pay arrangements, and struggling to negotiate the insecurity of potential deactivation and the risks of injury, sickness and other accidents at work (Rosenblat and Stark 2016, Scholz 2017, Schor and Attwood-Charles 2017, Cant 2019, Rosenblat 2019, Tassinari and Maccarrone 2020). These analyses deepened existing critiques of the platforms (for example, Morozov 2013, Slee 2015), and contradicted the more celebratory claims made in the management literature (for example, Botsman and Rogers 2010, Sundararajan 2016). Entire-home Airbnb listings were becoming more and more numerous, and gig work was leading to intensified forms of precarity. The 'sharing' metaphor was being further and further stretched.

Thus, in the same year as the European Commission's endorsement, articles by journalists and even prominent former advocates, while still minor voices as the wave of hype continued to rise in mainstream narratives, were already publicly expressing dismay about the ideas and concepts at the heart of these debates. Sarah Kessler's 2015 article 'The sharing economy is dead, and we killed it' and Joe Mathews' 2014 *Time* magazine article 'The sharing economy boom is about to bust' are also typical of commentary outside of the tech or business media since around 2015, in recapping, and rejecting, the seductive idea at the heart of the concept. Even a key figure from non-profit pro-sharing movement Ouishare, Sharing Economy luminary Arthur de Grave, wrote an article in 2016 entitled 'So long, collaborative economy!', admitting 'I just don't believe in it anymore'. The logic underpinning his initial approach, and the realisation of its limitations, remains illustrative for how the sector was and is still seen:

> For us, talking about the collaborative economy was above all, a bet for the future. Large platforms were of course rare and not always nice, but they were supposed to form a kind of vanguard: their success would be a prelude to the emergence of a motley crew of well-meaning initiatives. … And here, we strike the heart of the problem: I don't believe in it anymore. We've seen a lot of projects struggling to get by for a few years, and we've seen many more startups dying. And the big ones? They just kept growing. … The concept of the collaborative economy was composite by nature, from the beginning, but the tensions that shape it have reached a level today that makes it impossible to hold it together. We have to pull the plug. (De Grave 2016)

Commentators such as Slee, de Grave, Kessler and others argued that interest in alternative economic arrangements such as local currencies, cooperatives and time banks had been coopted, rather than mainstreamed or 'scaled up'. It was not only disappointment with the Sharing Economy that commentators and activists had begun to describe, but a disenchantment with the category itself; not only disillusionment that the Sharing Economy's benefits had not materialised, but a concern that buying into it as an idea had smoothed the way for the appropriation of progressive social movement framing and of social movement tactics. This position has been important for the development of more critical perspectives, and a wave of increasingly successful attempts at regulation.

The Sharing Economy idea, then, began to be questioned when employment rights issues and housing issues intensified and evidence became available about the links between them and the rise of platform businesses. Shortly afterwards, cheap credit started to dry up; return on investment began to matter; and prices rose. This shift has led to renewed calls for regulation, and renewed efforts by platform businesses to avoid it.

Platforms as disruption and avatars of progress: technological determinism and platform possibility

One of the key arguments of *Platform Politics* is that the core way that we understand technological change, and the future, has itself become a problem. This book is part of a growing body of research which presents a different type of explanation of the changes associated with platforms to dominant perspectives, both perspectives that are critical as well as those which are supportive. While this chapter argues that actors constantly frame, define and label platforms in ways which have shaped public debates, regulation and academic research, this section argues that rhetoric also shapes how we understand change and the future per se.

A range of debates relate platforms, transformation and the future. Lean platform businesses, as described in the previous section, are often presented in terms of their continuities with the wider political economic trend of neoliberalism, authors noting the longer-term historical shift towards deregulation, flexible workforces and increased rentier power. Some, in contrast, argue that the transformation around the platform economy can be characterised as a 'double movement' (Polanyi 2001), meaning that economic innovation moves in waves: platform corporations' destructive and destabilising activities generate regulatory and political responses which address some of the problems created (Cioffi et al 2022), with states expected to push back over the next decade. Some suggest that the platformisation of society is taking societies beyond capitalism altogether, where the elimination of ownership as a mode of property leads to a kind of 'techno-feudalism' (Morozov 2022, Varoufakis 2023), while the same forces, for others, indicate possible scenarios of abundance, democratic accountability and even luxury (Mason 2015, Frase 2016, Bastani 2019, Muldoon 2022). For the latter group, alternative platforms that are non-profit or which promise different types of economic exchange prefigure different possible futures of the platform economy (Scholz and Schneider 2017, Muldoon 2022).

However, more dominant than any of these narratives is another, fundamental to platform rhetoric, which needs to be confronted and unpacked. The story is in a popular genre commonly described as technological determinism, in which machines effectively transform society by directly altering the material conditions of existence. Platform businesses frame themselves, in claims that are widely repeated by mainstream commentary, as innovators and entrepreneurs, driving progress, modernisation and even civilisation itself. The argument is supported by the recent emergence of the businesses, their reliance on digital technology and the idea that technology, above all else, defines social relationships and the evolving nature of societies. These rhetorical claims have been involved in making cases for little, less or no regulation, while foreclosing any more radical intervention in governing and controlling platform services (for example, Muldoon 2022). This element of platform rhetoric has also dominated debates around technology giants Google, Amazon, Microsoft, Facebook/Meta and Microsoft, as well as self-driving cars, drones and artificial intelligence (Muldoon 2022; Morozov [2013] still provides the definitive discussion of early internet-related transformation).

Shoshana Zuboff's (2019: 222–226) discussion of digital technologies, looking beyond lean platforms, documents the use of these messages about technological determinism that she names *inevitabilism*. Inevitabilism is another way of describing the use of grandiose predictions by companies and their allies about technologically driven societal change that present a romanticised vision of their aspirations as a *fait accompli*. Companies such as Google, in other words, discuss their expansion as though there were no alternative, a position made possible by chief executive officers (CEOs) equating their own business with 'the internet' or 'the digital'. The message is also prevalent in management texts, literally exemplified in the title of *Wired* magazine's founding executive editor Kevin Kelly's (2016) influential book *The Inevitable: Understanding the 12 Technological Forces that will Shape Our Future*. Zuboff notes, however, that the rhetoric of inevitabilism, when successful, is performative. Despite the constant possibility of challenge, resistance and alternative pathways, narratives of inevitabilism attempt to 'convey the futility of opposition' (Zuboff 2019: 222) and 'protect power from challenge' (Zuboff 2019: 224). Zuboff argues that inevitabilism 'conceals the realpolitik of surveillance capitalism at work behind the scenes' (2019: 226), in other words, hiding the political struggles and sense of contingency that might come from acknowledging publicly the kind of interactions between movements, existing businesses, states and other actors.

This cluster of discursive tactics around change and the future is deployed by platforms publicly in media statements, speeches, websites, internal communications, and in public conversation with other actors, and it is widely reproduced by some business and technology commentators. Recourse to this narrative also offers opportunities not only to legitimise platforms, but to delegitimise antagonists. Legal, political and economic impediments to the operations of platform businesses such as regulation are thus generally presented as wrong-headed, heavy-handed, impracticable, unworkable, idiosyncratic, redundant and ignoring ordinary people's interests. Invoking enlightenment discourses to frame platform businesses as stewards of modernisation and progress allow for the critics of platforms to also be reframed as backward (although see the discussion and embrace of Luddite politics by figures such as Jathan Sadowski and Brian Merchant). Criticisms or attempts to regulate Uber, for example, are presented as critiques of contemporary digital technology and the logic of the internet per se; and thus, detractors of modernity and civilisation. These positions reproduce a popular neoliberal opposition between platform businesses (representing innovation and movement) and states (representing bureaucracy, inefficiency and vested interests). Often, this is refracted through a populist narrative suggesting that consumption of platform services provides a political or legal mandate for platforms' CEOs, framing a sovereign consumer represented by 'the people' as the protagonists facing regulation, rather than the businesses directly attempting to justify corporate misbehaviour.

In this vein, Brian Chesky, the CEO of Airbnb, speaking in 2014, describes struggles around regulation, and resistance to the company, simply as fear. Criticisms are recast as emotions. He also equates regulation with reactionary attitudes towards the internet per se – opposition towards which, even in 2014, would have widely been seen as unusual. The way that the idea of innovation becomes a rhetorical line of attack is illustrative.

> I understand why there are a lot of misconceptions. Airbnb is a really, really new idea. And I think we spent the last 15 or 20 years basically disrupting or changing the way content, bits, bytes, were suddenly consumed, interact, changed. But what happens when the internet started moving into your neighbourhood? With Airbnb, Uber, what happens when that actually happens? It starts to – well for some people they love it, but for other people they are very scared. … One thing I try to tell people is before you try to regulate something, just try to learn about it. … Thomas Jefferson said, in 1812, 'Laws and institutions must go hand in hand with the progress of the human mind. Institutions must advance also, and keep pace with the time'. If the government does not continue to regulate and update their law, and they're regulating 21st century businesses with 20th century laws, we could be in trouble. (Chesky 2014)

Platforms are not only the cutting edge of digital innovation; they also represent a rising tide of social and intellectual progress and enlightenment. From this perspective, it is easy for Chesky to frame resistance or state regulation as being antithetical to this modernisation meta-narrative. Quoting Thomas Jefferson, he suggests that standing in the way of tech giants might not only be an emotional and ignorant response, but it might be counter to civilisation and Americanism.

In such a way, platforms make the argument that existing regulation and legal frameworks are outdated, and new or proposed regulation is usually presented as over-complicated. These positions are used to justify operating outside and in spite of regulation, as suggested in Uber's remarkable Company Values, prior to their revision in 2017, one of which was 'Principled confrontation (Sometimes the world and institutions need to change in order for the future to be ushered in)' (Staley 2017).[3] Narratives about innovation contrast platforms' visionary approach with states and regulation. By representing and monopolising the future, platforms also implicitly deny the existence or possibility of other futures.

Finally, the technological determinism surrounding platform capitalism is so pervasive that it is even often part of the way that opposition to lean platforms is articulated. In other words, many critiques, though tending not to celebrate the changes associated with platforms, regularly still attribute these changes solely to platforms. In these narratives, platform capitalism is an example of the further intensification and sharpening of trends about capital accumulation. Power will tend to accrue to large companies through economies of scale as employment rights are eroded and inequality increases. State and business interests all but guarantee success for the rich and powerful. Elites become entrenched, and for some commentators, society risks moving towards a post-capitalist orientation that intensifies some of the worst trends in terms of precarity, a kind of dystopian techno-feudalism (for example, Morozov 2022, Varoufakis 2023). The sheer size of platforms (Lehdonvirta 2022), alongside difficulties with enforcement, is sometimes presented even by critics as though it made them invincible.

Platform Politics is concerned with an alternative genre of change to inevitabilism and technological determinism. It presents transformation as a process of negotiation, interaction and struggle, among platform businesses, states, social movements, international organisations, other corporations, platform users and alternative platform initiatives. This alternative genre takes all these protagonists seriously, treating platforms neither as heroes nor villains, but as internally contested and fallible collective actors, deploying tactics that are sometimes successful and sometimes unsuccessful.

The future of the platform economy is contingent. Platforms' rhetorical attempts to monopolise the future are a tactical wager. Their attempts to influence politicians and the public regularly backfire, and their efforts to mobilise their users and allies are increasingly coming under scrutiny. Activists, commentators and academics are developing alternative visions of how new digital technologies could be organised and governed (Scholz and Schneider 2017, Lehdonvirta 2022, Muldoon 2022, Varoufakis 2023). They suggest, noting the historical emergence of many initially privatised services, that platforms be democratised or nationalised, where popular control and ownership, not simply regulation, is established. As Schor and Vallas (2021) point out, this would represent a major shift in power relations, and as such requires political struggle and significant transformation in order to take place, as well as the formulation of alternatives. Yet, as the late Erik Olin Wright might have argued, that process has already begun: 'developing credible ideas about viable alternatives is one way of enhancing their achievability' (2010: 8).

Will economies of the future be algorithmically governed, state regulated, or coordinated and managed by the commons? Will our exchanges and interactions be shared and collaborative, and in what sense? What might these alternative socio-technical futures mean in practice? These are open questions: the future of the platform economy is up for grabs.

The Sharing Economy phrasebook: redefining and 'democratising' work, corporations, democracy

As discussed earlier, the idea of the Sharing Economy gave 'sharing' a particularly important role in tactics of platform rhetoric, becoming an increasingly polyvalent verb in the era of platform capitalism. It refers to renting, in the case of Airbnb; working, in the case of Uber and other gig economy companies; and supplying one's personal data to multinationals in the case of Facebook's 'sharing' of information (Kalamar 2013; see also Rosenblat 2019) – each of them useful euphemisms in the context of public opinion and legal struggles. The ideas are underpinned by a wider set of rhetorical tactics about the visions of the Sharing Economy inevitably becoming reality. This section explores how both these stories concern wider platform rhetorical tactics to redefine and rearticulate the meanings of work, the corporation and democracy.

The meaning of work is particularly important for 'gig economy' businesses such as ride-hailing and delivery platforms, where the argument that drivers and couriers are self-employed, legally, allows companies to avoid the costs associated with employment. The significance of this is obvious in the legal struggles that are taking place worldwide, but are also illustrated with the example of internal company communications for one meal delivery company. Thus, a leak from Deliveroo in 2017 revealed that it had created a guide for UK-based employees about how to discuss the company's couriers which resembled a foreign language phrasebook. Evidently, even company staff needed training to avoid using language referring to the delivery riders or drivers as workers or employees. The episode illustrates how platform businesses are engaged in an open epistemological struggle to redefine the core meanings of economic categories that extends even to internal documents and policies. Journalist Sarah Butler described the composition of the leaked 'Deliveroo phrasebook' in these terms:

A list of dos and don'ts setting out how to talk to the firm's food delivery riders, using terms that appear designed to fend off claims that they are employees. ... Couriers should always be referred to as 'independent suppliers' – self-employed workers with few employment rights – rather than as employees, workers, staff or team members ... riders do not clock on, but log in (to the rider app), and says that staff dealing with riders pay should always refer to invoices rather than payslips. … The company also provides handy example sentences:

Do say: Independent supplier, e.g. "We offer riders hours of work and they choose how many to accept based on their availability and the areas they want to work in."

Don't say: Employee/worker/staff member/team member, e.g. "Drivers are employed by Deliveroo to complete deliveries."

[…]

Do say: Termination, e.g. "We are terminating your Supplier Agreement due to your failure to meet Service Delivery Standards."

Don't say: Firing/sacking/resignation, e.g. "We are firing you due to poor performance." (Butler 2017)

Establishing a new language for Deliveroo employees to use is part of a wider strategy to reframe a debate that has serious consequences for employment rights and platform viability. The losses of lean platforms have so far significantly outstripped their profits,[4] meaning that they are reliant on continuing to grow; continuing to access cheap credit and labour, both now under threat; and maintaining a public image and a definition of work which protects their advantages. Meal delivery services, as with other platform work, describe their delivery riders or drivers as self-employed contractors, a legal category which entitles contractors to very few employment rights. This is sometimes referred to as the practice of *regulatory arbitrage*, which entails 'taking advantage of a gap between the economic substance of a transaction and its regulatory treatment' (Fleischer 2010: 230). In 2023 the company won the legal battle to avoid having to classify riders as workers in the UK, based on a Supreme Court ruling, suggesting some success in its approaches to redefine the employment relationship.

Platform businesses not only controversially define the nature of the relationship between themselves and platform workers, they also reframe the nature of their own existence, persistently downplaying their status as businesses, and the nature of their services. Metaphors and euphemisms are ubiquitous, again for purposes of regulatory arbitrage. Hence, for taxation and regulation purposes, lean platform companies claim to operate in a different sector to their competitors (for example, hotels and taxis), defining themselves as 'technology companies' or 'information society services', the latter suggesting that they are subject only to regulatory frameworks set up in the early 2000s to try to deal with media and information platforms (Tomassetti 2016, Aguilera et al 2025).[5] 'Information society service' is just one of a range of metaphors, some more technical, some more ephemeral, others more casual, and often used in combination, deployed by platform economy businesses to describe themselves.

For example, in Airbnb CEO Brian Chesky's TechCrunch speech in 2014 (see previous section), Chesky begins by describing the company as *an idea*, first ('I understand why there are a lot of misconceptions. Airbnb is a really, really new idea'), and subsequently as *a technology* – as, in fact, the internet itself ('But what happens when the internet started moving into your neighbourhood? With Airbnb, Uber, what happens when that actually happens?'). Both *ideas* and *technologies* evoke a story of innovation and advancement rather than the losses of housing, secure employment or other social harms that might be raised by the practices of lean platform business. Elsewhere, Chesky and other staff also refer to the company as a *community*, often framing the displeasure or concerns they feel themselves as being, rather, concerns of this community. The community are also invoked in Airbnb's staff's job titles, with hundreds of 'Community Organisers' created since 2013, and indeed the title 'Global Head of Community' created for businessman Douglas Atkin, who claims to have masterminded the company's corporate grassroots lobbying strategy (Slee 2015, Muldoon 2022). Sometimes, Airbnb statements even refer to the company as a 'movement', and occasionally even as 'the people' (see also Del Nido's [2021] discussion of Uber in Argentina).

In the context of struggles with governments, and in refusals by lean platforms to be regulated in the way that they want to be regulated (see Chapter 3) these arguments start to resemble what Nyberg and Murray (2023: 1) refer to as 'corporate populism', 'influenc[ing] democracies by constructing and reifying divisions in society, legitimizing depoliticization, and repressing representative democratic deliberations'. An example of Chesky reinterpreting basic words as part of a rhetorical argument for ignoring regulation established by political representatives is quoted in Stabrowski (2017: 327): 'There are laws for people and there are laws for business, but you are a new category, a third category – people as businesses. As hosts, you are micro-entrepreneurs and there are no laws written for micro-entrepreneurs.' In this way, lean platforms proliferate and legitimise an argument that existing laws do not apply to them.

Referring to Airbnb as a technology, idea, community or movement of micro-entrepreneurs denies a common-sense understanding of Airbnb as a company provisioning accommodation, to which any existing laws governing lodgings would apply. In turn, it obscures agency and sidesteps relationships of power among the constituencies: CEOs, workers; landlords ('hosts'), whether commercial or more casual; and customers or tenants ('guests'). Ignoring or fighting against regulation is no longer a business decision taken in order to satisfy investors and to eventually generate profit for shareholders, in spite of and versus democratically elected governments; rather, it is a movement of citizens or consumers voting with their feet against a clientelist elite. Thus, the idea of the platform as movement is important, *even before the platform users are mobilised as such.* Platforms 'pursuing a line of business in which changing the law is a significant part of the business plan' (Pollman and Barry 2016: 383) have obvious reasons to obscure who it is that is resisting or fighting unions, housing activists and regulators.

The *economic* nature of platform businesses, finally, is alternately downplayed, conflated with other characteristics and negated – important for lean platforms' political claim making. Niels Van Doorn (2020), building on Stabrowski (2017), thus notes a number of rhetorical 'slippages' between the economic and civic in his analysis of Airbnb. He examines the Airbnb Policy Tool Chest, intended for local governments to use as a template for regulation, and the company's corporate grassroots lobbying vehicle, Airbnb Citizen (see especially Chapter 5 for a full discussion and empirical examination of the practices of Airbnb Citizen). Van Doorn argues that Airbnb persistently frames the economic benefits of the platform for landlords in terms which suggest wider individual and societal benefits, using the terms 'empower', 'democratise' and 'citizen' in unconventional ways. By using Airbnb, hosts might simultaneously make money, establish friendships and learn to be entrepreneurs, while positively impacting their communities by encouraging increased and more equitably distributed tourism, providing services via the tax revenue generated. Economic gain and various communitarian and civic imaginaries are merged or treated as a win-win scenario.

> The main wager that Airbnb's Policy Tool Chest aims to communicate is that *platform-facilitated home sharing markets form the solution to a plethora of problems faced by cities and their inhabitants.* Its story, perfectly summarized in the document's cover note written by Chris Lehane – Airbnb's Global Head of Policy and Public Affairs and former Obama Administration official – is one of economic *and* civic empowerment (whereby the former fuels the latter) through tech-enabled, decentralized market-making. Besides 'economic opportunity,' the key term here is 'democratization': Airbnb ostensibly 'democratizes capitalism' by 'empowering people to use their homes to earn extra income' and thereby 'fostering entrepreneurship'; it allegedly also 'democratizes travel' by giving 'more people and more communities the opportunity to benefit from tourism's growth'; finally, it 'democratizes revenue' by generating 'new tax revenue that governments can dedicate to existing critical services' or use to invest in Airbnb-assisted 'new programs' that address local social challenges (Airbnb Citizen, 2016a). … Airbnb claims to make good on the promise of governance to establish economic efficiency and democratic legitimacy as two mutually enforcing policy goals. (Van Doorn 2020: 1813–1814, emphasis in the original)

Van Doorn's claims made around civic and economic empowerment and democracy are particularly interesting to discuss further. Democratisation, here, is about expanding not a civic but an economic franchise and means increased numbers of people who can consume a particular service. In Filip Stabrowski's (2017: 341) words, 'With the further intrusion of the market into the domestic sphere, Airbnb has linked the discourse of everyday entrepreneurialism with a higher civic purpose.'

If increased numbers of customers are understood as democratisation, this has also functioned as a threat, implicit or explicit, to policy makers who might wish to restrict or regulate the business. It strengthens the idea that the consumption of goods or services can be presented as political support for the company provisioning them: a consumer 'vote', similar to arguments about political and ethical consumerism (Culpepper and Thelen 2020), prior even to the mobilisation of users or allies. In one presentation, thus, Chris Lehane, then Head of Global Policy and Public Affairs at Airbnb, presents numbers of users of Airbnb, the 'Airbnb Community' – as though they were members of a political organisation (comparing to Sierra Club members; Human Rights Campaign members; the largest union in the United States, the National Education Association, and the National Rifle Association) (Alba 2015). Platform users are ventriloquised, even before their collective voice is generated using grassroots lobbying tactics. Through these moves, lean platforms frame political institutions who might like to regulate a business as *subverting democracy* (see Chan and Kwok 2021, Nyberg and Murray 2023). Claims about democracy, then, become doubly interesting when they are applied to platform power, explored in Chapters 4 and 5. With platform power, economic elites use civic repertoires to avoid regulation from democratically elected representatives that might compromise the democratisation of users conducting economic exchanges through platforms. In this way, Lehane also claimed that Airbnb's 'Host Clubs' were 'democratizing capitalism' (Dwoskin 2017).

Platform rhetoric reframes the concept of sharing and disruption, and it redefines employment, business and democracy. The latter idea, though, is most significant: it is about defending the idea that platform businesses, defined by their users, can speak for those users and other allies in political conflict with their business rivals, governments, housing activists and workers themselves. Platforms businesses argue that they are democratising democracy.

In recent years, the practices used by platforms to avoid regulation have themselves come under scrutiny. Forms of lobbying that have even less transparency than existing repertoires are becoming common. Regulators and the public mistake this mobilisation of platform users and allies, *platform power*, for independent movements and activists. We have little understanding of the relationships between lean platforms and the grassroots initiatives, an issue that is compounded in several ways by misleading platform rhetoric. In addition to the issues raised by housing and employment rights activists, therefore, there are now also many questions around the nature of corporate political activity practised by lean platforms.

Conflict, struggle, contingency: platform politics as an open struggle

Lean platforms are controversial for the problems associated with housing, employment, taxation and competition and, increasingly, their corporate political activity. Platforms attempt to smooth these tensions, and make sense of their growing power, by articulating and legitimating a new common sense about neoliberal capitalism, stories of inevitability and determinism, and redefining major categories of the economy and of politics such as employment, the corporation and democracy. The story of the growth of lean platforms, according to these arguments, is about modernisation, sharing and collaboration, progress, entrepreneurialism, and furthering the interests of the community.

In spite of the partial success of these arguments, however, lean platforms have provoked struggles around employment and labour issues; housing loss; additional urban pressures relating to tourism; unfair competition; social policy – with welfare benefits often tied to, and funded by, employment relationships; taxation policy; safety; and other indirect urban impacts such as increased congestion. Employment and labour issues and social policy concerns relate much more to the ride-hailing and delivery services such as Uber, Lyft, DiDi, Uber Eats, Deliveroo, Instacart and Doordash, as well as other labour platforms associated with the 'gig economy' such as cleaning and care services; while the main issues around housing and tourism are associated with short-term accommodation platforms; with the remainder, taxation and unfair competition, in particular, common to all.

Some of these controversies and tensions remain hidden from public view in some contexts, because they are debated or negotiated in the context of private lobbying, or the constituencies opposing platforms do not have traction in civil society or with the state. Tensions, conflicts and struggles also take many different forms, some more subtle than others. Many governments have welcomed platforms, regulating them in partnership with companies' own public policy teams, then letting the 'creative destruction' of existing industries ensue. Here, interactions and conflicts are latent, quickly resolved in favour of the platform businesses, often consolidating the impression that it is the latter who are the only agents of transformation. The tactic of simply arriving and scaling up rapidly, to 'ask for forgiveness, not permission' rests precisely on making it easier for governments to simply legalise existing practices without requiring changes in company practices (Del Nido 2021).

Yet the protests, blockades, subpoenas, occupations, lawsuits, petitions, fines from governments, strikes and boycotts recorded to date are visceral indicators that the consequences of lean platform businesses remain controversial in many contexts. Action by those most affected, and strikes by delivery companies such as Deliveroo, Uber Eats and Foodora drivers, for instance, have become common. Alternative platforms or initiatives have emerged, which often simultaneously present critiques while presenting more benign arrangements or arrangements which offset negative externalities, including an 'ethical' short-term rental service which seeks to involve local people in governing and benefiting from tourism (for example, Fairbnb), and cooperative models of platform taxi or food delivery services (for example, CoopCycle) who recognise working rights and distribute revenue among workers rather than shareholders (Baum 2018). These actions and initiatives, together, have led in turn to various attempts to regulate platform businesses, using a range of tools and approaches.

In direct contradiction to what platform rhetoric argues, *these actors and interactions matter*. Uber no longer exists in its initial form in some countries: in China, Turkey, Hong Kong, Taiwan, Hungary, Denmark, Norway, Germany, Spain and Switzerland, the company is either entirely absent or Uber drivers are simply licensed as taxi drivers, meaning there are few differences, in terms of pricing and organisation, with taxi services. While in the UK the Supreme Court recently upheld the definition of couriers suggested by meal delivery companies, the same court found that drivers for ride-hailing companies were employees. Uber's drivers in the UK are now paid minimum wage and accrue annual leave, although currently only for the period encompassing acceptance of a ride and the customer's arrival at a destination. In other contexts, meanwhile, Uber has replaced most taxi services, and it is even subsidised by public transport budgets in some jurisdictions (Calo and Rosenblat 2017). Airbnb has led to the transformation of millions of housing units into short-term lettings worldwide, yet further growth is restricted now in a small number of European and North American cities (Cox and Haar 2020), with absolute numbers recently diminishing in several such contexts (Colomb and Moreira de Souza 2023). The European Union's Platform Work Directive, passed in 2024, included a legal 'presumption of employment', which, while it does not mean that platform workers in the European Union automatically become employees, obliges member states to establish the criteria which trigger the presumption of that employment (European Parliament 2024). The variation in outcomes contradicts accounts of inevitability; differences reveal contingency. The next chapter examines the dynamics of interaction and conflict which lead to these different outcomes.

From platform rhetoric to regulatory struggle

This chapter has been about examining the *context* of platform struggles and *platform rhetoric* at the general level, fundamental for our understanding of what the problem and what the regulatory solutions might. Platform businesses are engaged in an open epistemological conflict to redefine the core meanings of economic categories and political processes in order to protect their regulatory advantages. The questions of whether the drivers and riders delivering meals and transporting passengers are employees of platforms or freelancers, and whether short-term lettings platforms provision accomodation or are simply intermediaries, are existential – platforms sometimes decide to leave contexts where they cannot make their rhetoric stick in the legislature. The arguments, however, go beyond redefining what platforms are, what they do and what their relationship is with their different users. They extend, due to their significance for regulation, to arguments about democracy and political processes. Platforms, argue platforms, democratise services, casting regulators as subverting democracy: this appears to pitch consumption against citizenship as political practices, even prior to the mobilisation of the users of platform companies.

Given the centrality of platform businesses to the 'new common sense' of neoliberal capitalism (Srnicek 2016), to question the legitimacy of the platform economy, and to attempt to regulate, now means to challenge the new post-crash capitalist orthodoxy. In the context of these problems, activists have begun to question the legitimacy of the businesses that have been, for some years, one of the most popular and appealing faces of corporate power. The question of the legitimation of the platform economy, and the possibility of its being addressed societally, then, is also about the legitimacy of neoliberalism and capitalism per se, and the extent to which society might be able to reshape these fundamental processes. We should worry about lean platforms because they not only erode employment rights and housing stocks, but also because they are challenges to society's capacity to govern corporations, and the right of ordinary people to shape the conditions of their environments, their economic reality, and their everyday lives. The next chapter looks at the dynamics of these struggles around regulation, before a wider investigation of the tactics that the businesses have employed in Chapters 4 and 5.

3

Trajectories of Struggle around Lean Platforms: Making Sense of Change

The corporate political activity of lean platforms in context

As discussed, the stories platform businesses tell about themselves, their users and their own corporate political activity creates confusion about their power, their relationship to neoliberal capitalism and the process by which they have grown. This chapter presents a contrasting perspective to these narratives, collecting and reviewing the empirical evidence of the conflicts and struggles that have accompanied processes of transformation, and identifying the common political processes and tactical approaches used. It shows that the form that platform businesses eventually take in any given context depends on interactions and conflicts between platforms, other businesses, lobbyists, states, investors, critical social movements, non-corporate platform alternatives, media, and the users and customers of platforms. These struggles are still ongoing and are at very different stages in different places.

A range of business tactics have been deployed to protect the legislative and fiscal advantages lean platforms hold over traditional hotels, taxi firms and other competitors. They include many forms that are recognisable from the extant literature on corporate political activity (for example, Katic and Hillman 2023), including private lobbying; lawsuits, appeals and legal threats; refusal to follow local laws; threats to leave a jurisdiction; withholding data required to enforce laws; incentivising law-breaking to prevent enforcement; offers of collaboration, negotiation and self-regulation; 'business model adaptation' involving linguistic and legal contortions to avoid their business falling under certain regulatory frameworks; 'venue shifting' to get local policies overturned by other authorities; framing and messaging tactics to shape public perception and influence law-makers; public relations (PR) strategies that involve the mobilisation of users or allies in order to shape public perception and influence law-makers, consultations or referenda; PR strategies to create mobilisation arrangements with allies; rapid expansion or 'blitzscaling', using heavy incentives to ensure popular buy-in from users (introductory offers for customers and drivers, hosts and other intermediaries); and delaying tactics – whether legal or relating to negotiation, which also allow the company to consolidate its position as a normal part of life and the economy in the society in question, making further disruption by the state less attractive a prospect. This chapter describes how these tactics become part of common platform political strategies across platforms and contexts.

The focus on these tactical elements is not to suggest that they are the only approaches taken. Lean platforms also practise the full repertoire of corporate political activity, the range of which is usefully summarised by Katic and Hillman (2023). They also include, therefore, contributions to the campaigns of politicians or parties, advocacy advertising, commissioning research projects and reporting results, political connections, PR, press conferences, market actions such as firm location decisions or collaboration on government projects, regulatory co-creation with government, self-regulation, regulatory framing, litigation, commenting on proposed regulations, dormancy (temporarily reducing operations to wait for political opportunities to change), performing favours for politicians, 'geopolitical jockeying' where firms capitalise on the historical and aspirational attributes of national identity, and corporate activism (where firms speak or act on controversial sociopolitical issues). Most of these activities are mentioned in the platform regulation literature, but they are more familiar stories of corporate power, and although lean platforms engage in particularly extensive direct lobbying and campaign contributions, relative to their size (see Collier et al [2018] for a useful breakdown of Uber's tactics in the US context), we know a disproportionate amount about these processes from existing scholarship. As Katic and Hillman (2023) note, literature on corporate political activity is dominated by research on these tactics, meaning that there is an increasingly widely acknowledged need to catalogue and empirically research newer, more informal and more indirect tactics such as platform power. This, and the innovations made by lean platforms in their political activity, justifies further attention to a subset of practices of corporate political activity that appear to play an outsized role in the legitimation of lean platforms and their particular forms of expression of neoliberal corporate power.

Thus, literature on platform regulation has noted the significance of *platform rhetoric*, and the distinctive approaches to corporate grassroots lobbying which we call *platform power*, approaches that are generally used together (on Uber see especially Collier et al 2018, Rosenblat 2018, Thelen 2018, Tzur 2019,

Chan and Kwok 2021, Seidl 2022; on Airbnb see especially Stabrowski 2017, 2022, Aguilera et al 2019). These tactics, which I characterise in this chapter as being about *politicisation* through *framing and mobilisation*, are flanked by two other sets of practices. The first of these, which I refer to as *incursion, expansion and habituation*, is designed to make regulatory challenge undesirable in the first place, and sets the groundwork for fighting any potential challenge: unannounced arrival to a jurisdiction, typically through rapid expansion and integration in users' everyday lives. The other, referred to broadly as *inhibiting enforcement*, is a repertoire of ongoing tactics that allow companies to evade existing or new regulation once established as relevant, especially through *withholding data, stalling, non-cooperation, and venue-shifting* (see, for example, Cox and Haar 2020, Colomb and Moreira de Souza 2023, Mazur and Serafin 2023).

The main argument is that despite contextual differences and differences in the issues and themes raised by different businesses, these are common approaches to legitimation and regulatory evasion. These common trajectories are identified through reviewing extant analyses of the regulation of platforms. Some of that analysis has been comparative (Collier et al 2018, Rosenblat 2018, Thelen 2018, Uzunca et al 2018, Aguilera et al 2019, Chan and Kwok 2021), and some draws on more detailed location-specific case studies (for example, Stabrowski 2017, 2022, Del Nido 2021, Seidl 2022).[1] Each strand identifies part of the process through which platforms become politicised in the first place; how, when and why platforms are regulated; and what patterns there are in these struggles. The academic literature remains concentrated on the two biggest lean platform sectors, those also responsible for the greatest revenue: ride-hailing and short-term lettings platforms, and the market leaders in each – Uber and Airbnb – but increasingly, other platforms are being analysed in analogous terms. Political dynamics of food delivery platforms have so far played out in direct struggles between riders and drivers and the businesses themselves (see, for example, Cini et al 2022, Woodcock and Cant 2022, Vrikki and Lekakis 2023), often at a local but also sometimes national level, meaning that these platforms play only a small role in the comparison that follows, although meal delivery services are included in the analysis of Chapters 4 and 5. Little scholarship so far analyses the struggles around other platforms, in part because they entered into already highly informal sectors, but increasingly scholars are gathering empirical data about the dynamics of care and cleaning work (for example, Ticona et al 2018, Ticona 2022, Koutsimpogiorgos et al 2023), micromobility (for example, Stehlin and Payne 2023) and the variety of forms of labour associated with platforms such as Taskrabbit and Amazon Turk (see, for example, Lehdonvirta 2022). It remains to be seen how far these platforms replicate the patterns identified in this chapter.

Incursion, expansion, habituation: the basis of platform struggle

The first common element identified in work examining the trajectories around political struggle has been the initial approach by platform businesses, and the early interactions that take place at this point. Lean platforms normally launch abruptly, an *incursion* disregarding existing regulation, allowing rapid *expansion*, funded by vast amounts of venture capital enabled by cheap credit, prior to and during legal and political challenges, and *habituation* – establishing large numbers of users via incentives and convenient software that integrate platform services into people's everyday lives as customers, workers or landlords. *Incursion* and *habituation* are both terms also used by Shoshana Zuboff (2019) to describe two of four processes used by media platforms (especially Google and Facebook) to extract data in what she calls 'accumulation by dispossession', a process by which companies take ownership and economically exploit people's personal data (Zuboff 2019: 137–174). She stylises incursion as the launch of an approach by a company which proceeds until resistance is encountered 'without authorisation, knowledge, or agreement' (Zuboff 2019: 140). Although there are other parallels with the subsequent processes Zuboff identifies among the data platforms she studies, noted throughout, the trajectories of lean platforms have their own additional processes and tactics revealed by the wider literature and my findings.

Multiple authors find the process of *incursion*, albeit using diverse terms, important for their analysis of Uber. Ruth Collier and colleagues (2018), Rosenblat (2018) and Thelen (2018) all highlight the importance of the nature of Uber's initial arrival in their outstanding comparative analyses of the company's divergent regulatory trajectories across numerous city and state contexts in the United States; the United States and Canada; and the United States, Sweden and Germany, respectively. Collier et al (2018: 922–923) notes that Uber launches in a new jurisdiction, 'ignoring an extensive regulatory regime, which includes, among other provisions, barriers to entry and price controls; driver registration, licensing, and insurance requirements; and /consumer protection and safety regulations'. Cities and states frequently lack the resources or staff to enforce these regulations, which are disregarded by the lean platforms using the justification of their self-identification as technology platforms (see Chapter 2).

Rosenblat (2018) also highlights the need for lean platforms to build relationships with users immediately – *habituation* – with generous wage incentives to drivers and subsidised rides to consumers offered, creating a 'self-reinforcing cycle of increased supply (of drivers) and increased demand (by users)' (Thelen 2018: 941), driving *expansion*. Increased numbers of drivers reduce wait times dramatically, improving the service, while increased numbers of customers mean more reliable and lucrative earnings, especially immediately after launch, as ride-hailing and delivery companies tend to subsequently reduce driver rates (see, for example, Rosenblat 2018, Del Nido 2021). These allow platform services to become integrated into daily lives and habits of work, travel and consumption, which come to depend on the mediation of platforms (Valdez 2023). A similar emphasis on rapidly scaling up in urban contexts has also been noted in discussions of short-term lettings platforms, food delivery services, scooters and bike-sharing schemes. While the processes with many of these platforms have not yet been well documented in the academic literature, Murray Cox and Kenneth Haar (2020), among others, note a similar challenge with Airbnb's launch in a city, and its implications for the governance of the platform in the moment, and in the future:

When short-term rental platforms arrived, the only public face of a short-term rental property became an anonymous digital listing with only an approximate location of the property with an unverified first name of the host. The anonymous nature of a digital short-term rental listing makes it extremely difficult for local agencies to enforce their local zoning, building, tourist and housing laws. This is compounded by the exponential increase of demand for short-term rental properties, including aggressive marketing to potential hosts or property investors, resulting in hundreds or thousands of new properties entering the short-term rental market, many without going through the steps to verify if the activity is allowed, or notifying the city. (Cox and Haar 2020: 12)

The speed and scale of the habituation and expansion process is made possible by a particular political economic model (see also the section 'The Sharing Economy reflects the crisis' in Chapter 2). It is an approach that is, in the tech world and beyond, also heavily freighted with ideology, being familiarly referred to using slogans of platform chief executive officers, such as 'move fast and break things' (Facebook's Mark Zuckerberg) and 'don't ask permission, ask forgiveness' (Uber's Trevor Kalanick). It is funded by a 'growth first' or 'blitzscaling' (Hoffman and Yeh 2018) business model, an approach that, already building on a distinctive business culture in Silicon Valley, is enabled by an era of unprecedentedly cheap credit, a normalisation of aggressive expansion in the tech sector and in investor circles, especially obvious with Amazon, and the idea that efficiency can be compromised initially in order to benefit from the 'network effects', infrastructural leverage (Valdez 2023) and then monopoly power of dominating a market. Expansion and habituation are two parts of the same process, involving channelling significant investment into establishing as big a user base as possible, destroying local competition and giving the companies economic and political leverage for regulatory struggles. They are reliant on continued investor confidence, and a strong relationship between the business and its users whereby a service becomes part of the everyday lives of workers, landlords and customers.

Incursion, and the accompanying processes of rapid *expansion* and everyday *habituation* of the services, creates the conditions for the weaponising of convenience in the event of political struggle, as the next section discusses. As Collier et al (2018: 922) point out in their analysis of Uber in North America, the approach of incursion, integration and expansion 'forces local or state governments to respond reactively to a fait accompli, after Uber has established a base of customers and drivers'. This means that almost immediately, authorities are faced with a choice of banning platform services, risking the livelihoods of those who may be already dependent on the work and infrastructure, and the anger of the app's users; or allowing it to continue to rapidly expand, making future regulation that might limit the company (vehicle caps for Uber and neighbourhood-specific numbers of short-term lets for Airbnb, for example) even more difficult to countenance, and enforcement even more challenging.

Politicisation, framing and mobilisation: how platforms are problematised and how they respond

Lean platforms' common tactical approach to abrupt *incursion*, in particular relying on rapid *expansion* and everyday *habituation* of the service in the lives of workers and consumers, are the basis for continuing to grow revenue, to attract further investment and to establish the basis of a local monopoly or part of a small oligopoly that may allow for eventual profits. They are also the basis of platform business tactics for dealing with potential challenges. These challenges might arise from the non-compliance of platforms with existing regulations (as argued, incursion usually involves disregarding any that might exist), attempts at enforcement of these regulations, or proposals for new regulations, which might limit the further growth of platforms. These processes around challenges are about *politicisation, framing* and *mobilisation*. They refer to the problematising of platforms by various actors, the debate about what the issues are and the emergence of a campaign or programme to address them, which in the case of lean platforms is frequently met with counter-mobilisations, coordinated by the platform itself.

The politicising, problematising or questioning of a lean platform business has taken more forms than might be supposed. Particularly early on, each lean platform business model was challenged in several ways, which were highly variable and especially dependent on institutional and contextual differences. While the sharpening of critical debates has led to some homogenisation in this respect, a central early finding has been that these issues, or the way that platform businesses and their externalities have been *framed*, are pivotal both for the nature of regulation and for its success. Aguilera and colleagues (2019), for example, compare regulation of Airbnb, identifying processes of politicisation and regulatory outcomes in three European cities, as part of an important comparative project which examines nine more cities and their regulation through key stakeholder interviews (see also Colomb and Moreira de Souza 2021, 2023, Aguilera et al 2025). In their words: 'Three main factors emerge from the comparison to explain the variations in the regulations: the type of actors who politicized the issue in the first place; the distribution of competences between scales of government; and the existing instruments available to the city administration' (Aguilera et al 2019: 12).

Aguilera et al (2019) suggest that much depends on the actors who initially *mobilised* against the platform business – as these commonly frame the problem in subsequent debates (see also Rosenblat 2018, Thelen 2018, Seidl 2022), suggest potential allies for both the policy maker and the business (see also Thelen 2018), and often define what regulatory tools are available to the policy maker. Policy makers at any one scale, as Aguilera et al (2019) note, have only limited powers, and local, regional, national and supranational policy makers need to be supportive for them to be workable longer term, and are often played off against each other (see the practices of *inhibiting enforcement*, as discussed in this chapter). The empirical data gathered by Aguilera et al (2019) show that in Barcelona, social movements critical of tourism problematised short-term lets, whereas in Paris it was policy makers working in housing; while in Milan, the main actors to *politicise* short-term lets were Sharing Economy advocates, whose aim was to foster economic growth and social inclusion, with short-term lettings platforms seen as a strong potential catalyst for both. Aguilera et al (2019) are actually making two important points about politicisation here. One is about which actors are mobilised, and therefore the possibilities of different campaigns or alliances which might regulate or re-regulate. The other point is about how the issue is presented, framed and represented culturally – allowing different possibilities for more or less salient issues to the local context to be referenced in order to generate public support for the regulatory measures, if the regulator is successful, or disquiet and opposition if they are not. Some of the arguments made by Airbnb in these debates are context-specific, some are sector-specific, and many invoke broader arguments about innovation and technological change (see Chapters 1 and 2). In each case, however, Aguilera and colleagues (2019) not only raise the issue of *politicisation* and issue *framing*, but also *mobilisation*: the movements challenging tourism in Barcelona, such as the Association for Sustainable Tourism; the Milanese pro-Sharing movement; the mobilisation of Airbnb's users individually; and the creation of new groups created and/or supported by the corporation (see Chapters 4 and 5). 'Airbnb has developed new strategies of political influence based on the mobilization of the platform's individual users, who are encouraged to mobilize against attempts to regulate the sector – collectively via the above-mentioned "home-sharing clubs" and the platform's dedicated policy website (airbnbcitizen.com), and individually via "protest" e-mails pre-drafted by Airbnb' (Aguilera et al 2019: 19–20).

The processes of *politicisation, framing* and *mobilisation* are also highly salient for making sense of Uber's regulation. Seidl's (2022) longitudinal analysis in New York City demonstrates how platform businesses and their problems were initially politicised and framed, followed by an analysis of the changes and their outcomes. In 2015, an attempt by then-mayor Bill de Blasio to impose a cap in the city, justified by the issue of congestion, failed to mobilise wider groups around, for example, disability rights or workers' rights. Uber were able to frame the issue as being about the exclusion of racially minoritised people and racial inequality, presenting de Blasio as having sided with the establishment (licensed taxi drivers). This allowed the company to establish a 'wedge coalition', which, despite de Blasio's overwhelming legislative power, split his Democrat councillors and separated him from much of his voter base. In 2018, by contrast, Seidl (2022) argues, de Blasio was successful in framing the issue of the need for a cap in terms of workers' rights, a much more resonant narrative, meaning that the story about exclusion and inequality that Uber told was much less effective.

There is also variation across cities within the same national contexts for both Uber and Airbnb (Benli-Trichet and Kübler 2022), and there are also differences internationally, as demonstrated by Thelen (2018). Thelen shows that one way in which variation emerges in trajectories of regulation across Sweden, Germany and the United States, where outcomes have been very different, was around how Uber triggered conflict over different issues that were important for different groups. Thelen shows a strong relationship between the complaints and claims made against the company with the narratives subsequently used in media outlets to describe the disputes, and subsequent processes and regulatory outcomes at the time of writing. The range of complaints raised included unfair competition (from established taxi and transportation companies), employment and labour issues (whether drivers should be considered employees and eligible for benefits accordingly, or, as Uber argues, independent contractors or freelancers), social policy (where benefits are contingent on or are financed by actual employment), taxation policy and consumer safety (Thelen 2018: 943). In Germany, unfair competition was seen as the main issue, which meant that a rapid injunction was called by the national mobile taxi hailing company, and an early decision in a Frankfurt state court effectively banned Uber across all of Germany, whereas consumer safety and employment issues had tended to dominate discussions in the United States, which, partly because of jurisdictional fragmentation, led to very light moderation. Meanwhile, taxation and social policy were seen as much more significant challenges in Sweden, leading to a response Thelen characterises as 'adaptation' (for a further comparison between Sweden and other Nordic countries see Oppegaard et al 2020). Again, as in Aguilera and colleagues' (2019) discussion of Airbnb, different issues mobilised particular actors and triggered variations in the strategic repertoire of the company. 'Uber triggered conflicts over different regulatory issues in different national (or local) contexts. As a result, it mobilised different actors ... and it inspired the formation of different alliances' (Thelen 2018: 942).

Thelen (2018), like Seidl (2022), and indeed all the authors examining the regulation of platforms, also draws particular attention to the mobilisation of users and/or allies as a pivotal tactic which works alongside framing or storytelling, in placing pressure on elected policy makers through public opinion, whether real or anticipated. In the United States, Uber, hence, was able to establish strong relationships with Democrats and Republicans at the national level, with the company symbolising different issues or frames simultaneously: 'Prominent republicans heralded Uber as a champion of free markets, while democrats (with an eye toward their millennial base) embraced it as urban, progressive, and innovative' (Thelen 2018: 945).

> In sum, in a context in which conflicts over Uber have played out in decentralised and highly politicised venues, Uber has been able to inspire competition across jurisdictions and play on politicians' fears of appearing hostile to technology. Most importantly, by organising its users and mobilising them as a political weapon, the company largely succeeded in isolating its main competitor, local taxi companies. (Thelen 2018: 945)

The mobilisation of opponents and users in platform power is a key element of Thelen's (2018) explanation, mirroring other analysis (for example, Collier et al 2018, Uzunca et al 2018, Serafin 2019, Chan and Kwok 2021). In Germany, 'coordinated action by established taxi providers interfered with Uber's ability to recruit drivers and build up sufficient supply to drive prices down ... a dearth of drivers meant Uber users experienced long wait times for a ride' (Thelen 2018: 946). While in the United States Uber 'picked off cities one at a time', the coordination of German taxi operators led to a very different outcome. In Sweden, meanwhile, Thelen characterises the case as 'adaptation' involving concessions from Uber and some deregulation of taxi services per se. There, contestation revolved around establishing new taxation agreements rather than challenging Uber drivers' employment status, largely because existing taxi firms did not directly employ drivers anyway, meaning that taxi drivers only partially mobilised. Interestingly, different political institutions and political economic systems afford very different possibilities for mobilisation. Chan and Kwok's (2021) brilliant discussion of Uber's regulation in China, Hong Kong and Taiwan attributes most of the differences in outcomes to narratives and frames made by the company which relate directly to mobilisation and public opinion: in Taiwan Uber's approach was 'relatively more effective in the democratic context because the firm could successfully mobilize the fictitious voice of the citizens to legitimize its business' (Chan and Kwok 2021: 780).

Prominent examples of these uses of political participation techniques around *mobilisation* alongside *framing* are identified in all contexts examined, including, for example, the UK (Andrews 2017), China, Hong Kong and Taiwan (Chan and Kwok 2021), Netherlands, the UK and Egypt (Uzunca et al 2018), Poland (Serafin 2019), among others, while Cox and Haar (2020) and Stabrowski (2017, 2022) show that similar combinations of framing and user mobilisation are used by Airbnb in over a dozen European and North American cities in addition to those examined by Aguilera et al (2019, 2025). Yet, the mobilisation of users and allies depicted in these accounts appears to take several different forms. Even within Collier et al's (2018) discussion of regulatory disruption in cities, state legislatures and judicial venues in the United States, for example, several distinctive approaches seem to involve such mobilisation and framing. They highlight the formation of alliances with non-profit groups, alliances with other actors such as insurance companies, clicktivism, online petitions, referenda, PR campaigns and manipulation of public opinion data, all mentioned in media and academic discussions of other contexts. They target a range of users and allies, or potential allies – often existing grassroots actors. While these are relatively low-cost forms of action, Chan and Kwok (2021) note that Uber even organised demonstrations of drivers in the context of Taiwan. Aguilera et al's (2019, 2025) discussion of Airbnb, and trade union UGT's (2021) discussion of meal delivery platforms in Spain, suggests that new groups of users are created and mobilised by platforms, approaches which are both more demanding in terms of commitment required from users, and longer term in their nature (see Chapters 4 and 5). Collier et al (2018), finally, also note the combination of mobilisation and framing with other tactics: threats to leave markets, direct lobbying and strategic use of celebrities to target certain politicians.

Mobilisation tactics not only combine with frames in interesting and context-specific ways in all these examples, but they also vary in their approaches in several other respects. Sometimes they appear to mobilise users directly, whereas sometimes they make existing grassroots groups partners. Sometimes customers are mobilised, but other groups are too: drivers, riders and hosts. Some initiatives seem to be temporary or very short-term – the signing of a petition or contacting of a representative, for example – whereas some appear to be campaigns or the establishing of a new constituency – the clubs set up by Airbnb or the rider groups created by meal delivery companies in Spain. These differences and gaps in the literature are returned to in Chapters 4 and 5, where an extended example of platform mobilisation is presented, and the practices involved in these forms of mobilisation are catalogued and typologised. Before that, however, a third overarching set of repertoires that are key for the regulatory trajectories of lean platforms are described.

Inhibiting enforcement: non-cooperation, withholding data, stalling and venue-shifting

The third and final constellation of processes centre on the regulatory process, explaining how relevant regulation is not always enough in itself. It focuses on enforcement, and the tactics which inhibit enforcement of existing or new laws. Inhibiting enforcement takes several forms, including general *non-cooperation* with laws and threats to leave jurisdictions; *withholding data*; the use of *stalling* or delay tactics by platform businesses to slow down state processes while platforms continue to expand rapidly; and *venue-shifting*, where businesses target different legislative arenas – seeking advantage by initially engaging with certain regulatory entities or institutions, then seeking to overturn undesired outcomes by moving to a different scale of government or a different regulatory domain. As Jimena Valdez (2023: 178) puts it pithily, 'regulation is not the end of the story'.

Platform businesses can be highly uncompromising, intransigent and chaotic agents to regulate. Existing sanctions or fines set up to penalise misbehaviour may be designed for small businesses and infractions, so if applied to platform businesses can be paid easily by platforms, and challenged legally, to further delay processes. Sometimes, enforcement targets platform users such as short-term-let landlords, and platforms have sometimes supported these users legally. In each of these cases, following incursion, where platforms enter markets extra-legally, ignoring existing regulatory frameworks, there are a variety of seemingly official and less official, or guerilla, tactics used by the platforms, or platforms and their users together, which continue to create enforcement difficulties even in the case of a successful regulatory initiative emerging from the processes of politicisation, framing and mobilisation.

Cox and Haar (2020) provide a detailed list of Airbnb's repertoire of these tactics around inhibiting enforcement:

- Hiding identities of hosts and locations of illegal listings
- Systematically fail to verify host identities and locations
- Refuse to follow local laws like displaying registration numbers or removing illegal listings

- Threatening legal action over new regulations and filing abusive lawsuits
- Refusing to provide data for enforcement
- Failing to disclose activity for taxes collected
- Using taxes to avoid housing regulations
- Offering negotiation to avoid regulations (spoiler, most negotiations fail)
- Withdrawing negotiated agreements in retaliation [for enforcement of regulations]
- Self regulation tools: trivial to bypass (yearly caps and 'one host one home')
- Proposing ineffective regulations to delay and block better regulations. (Cox and Haar 2020: 3)

While a few of these tactics are about making regulation difficult in the first place, nearly all are about inhibiting enforcement that is proposed or pending. Some tactics are direct: hiding identities of hosts and illegal listings; systematically failing to verify them; refusing to follow local laws; *withholding data* for enforcement; failing to disclose activity for taxes collected; and forms of *non-cooperation*, such as threatening to leave a jurisdiction. And others are much more about slowing the process down or *stalling*: Cox and Haar (2020) note that the experiences of policy makers is that the negotiations frequently offered by Airbnb tend to amount to little or no progress because the company will not agree to anything that threatens its business model: likewise, they argue, self-regulation tools, proposing ineffective regulations and threatening legal action all seem designed to either encourage policy makers to give up regulating altogether, or slow the process down – meanwhile allowing Airbnb to continue to expand, develop relationships with users and hence build up its mobilisation leverage.

Stalling is the flipside to platforms' rapid expansion, and a fundamental element of nearly all the trajectories examined in the literature, though it has only recently been framed as a tactical approach in its own right. Mazur and Serafin (2023) point out, deploying the example of Uber in Poland, that recognising stalling as a tactic challenges the narrative of technological innovation that implies that platforms are simply quicker, more progressive or ahead of the state in some fundamental way. 'While it is often claimed that the pace of digital transformation is such that its own, often glacial changes do not allow the state to catch up, we argue that technological companies, with the help of some state actors, have been slowing the state down' (Mazur and Serafin 2022: 101). They note that this tactic works hand-in-hand with the continued expansion of the business and accumulation of 'platform power'. There are several advantages to the tactic:

Stalling creates time for technological lock-in to set in, which increases the economic costs of switching to a different platform or going off platform altogether. It also creates time for institutional deepening, enabling the platform to establish legitimacy (Serafin, 2019; Adler, 2021), permeate social relations, and become an infrastructure to everyday practices and beliefs. A digital platform profits not only because it is able to use the time earned through stalling to generate revenue but also because it can use this time to grow, learn about consumers, improve its services, lobby, delegitimize existing regulation, and accumulate platform power. For a digital platform, growing and accumulating platform power facilitates future profitmaking by improving its structural position vis a vis any potential competitor (Muennich, 2019). It leads to the 'institutionalization of advantage' (Pierson, 2016, p. 131). But growing and accumulating platform power also makes the platform more difficult to regulate due to policymakers' growing fear of opposing a company that has become a basic infrastructure in the lives of many of their constituents. Moreover, as we shall show in the case of Facebook later, once a platform has accumulated platform power it continues to use stalling strategies as a defensive strategy during scandals, which as Culpepper and Thelen point out (2020), threaten the platform–consumer alliance at the heart of platform power. (Mazur and Serafin 2023: 105–106)

Mazur and Serafin (2023) elaborate five stalling tactics, most of which are visible across numerous individual case studies and comparisons:

1. *making time by reinventing classifications*: platform companies' claims about their identity as technology companies during incursion – see the section on 'Incursion, expansion, habituation: the basis of platform struggle' and Chapter 2;
2. *stealing time from street-level bureaucrats*, for example Uber's use of the Greyball app to create fake drivers to foil law enforcement operations, and swamping institutions with freedom of information/public records requests about enforcement processes, also used against opponents, as in platform companies' harassment of critical US academic Veena Dubal during the Proposition 22 campaign; see Hiltzik (2020);
3. *dragging out court proceedings* – they describe the examples of advising hosts or drivers to reject fines and go to court, offering to pay fines or legal fees, coordinating their defences, and systematically forcing cases to be postponed by engineering deliberate irregularities;
4. *delaying new regulations*, often by agreeing with the proposed need for regulation but criticising various elements of proposals and suggesting further dialogue or consultation, or extending transitional periods between the passing of a law and its taking effect; and
5. *taking time to (not) comply*, as in introducing new contracts which appear to legally dodge new regulation while not fundamentally changing anything.

While the stalling approaches identified by Mazur and Serafin are useful, the language of *stalling* suggests that a temporal dynamic in which regulation is eventually made possible. On occasion, however, the approaches listed are simply attempts to avoid regulation altogether, not just slow it down.

An additional tactic for inhibiting enforcement, not mentioned by Mazur and Serafin, yet which in some circumstances may be a sixth stalling approach, has been *withholding data* needed for regulation: the deliberate hiding and obfuscation of information held or gathered by platforms that is required to assess the impacts of a platform business, or to enforce its regulation. Multiple authors are finding that the control over data held by platform businesses allows them to hide illegal activity and make its prevention highly resource-intensive, meaning that any effective regulation tends to mandate the sharing of data. The significance of data in these struggles is obvious from the problems around enforcement, but also simply in understanding whether regulation is necessary or what is even going on with respect to platforms, even what platforms are (see Chapter 2), as well as the nature and accuracy of their claims and the work underpinning their platform power initiatives (Chapters 4 and 5). This attempt to monopolise data has meant that the public and governments have been hindered in their attempts to understand the scale of the platforms and their effects. This was particularly true of Airbnb, where in contrast to drivers or couriers, landlords – whether they hold several properties or conform to the original but increasingly elusive figure of the 'home-sharer' – have tended to share an interest in the platform operating under the radar, as it reduces the risk of their illegal lettings being targeted by enforcement. That has meant that data scraping from academics and data activists, such as those running the not-for-profit Inside Airbnb project, have become enormously important.

A final additional approach to inhibiting enforcement common to platform businesses that needs to be highlighted is *venue-shifting*. Airbnb, for example, regularly addresses resistance from authorities or movements by taking up political struggles at different scales (Aguilera et al 2019: 17), with the company recently lobbying the European Commission to overturn local city-level regulation (Corporate Europe Observatory 2018, Cox and Haar 2020, Colomb and Moreira de Souza 2021, Aguilera et al 2025). A similar move has been identified by Collier et al (2018), Thelen (2018), Baron (2018) and Occhiuto (2021) with respect to Uber. This might mean shifting from municipal to regional or national scales to try and overturn legislation, or it might mean shifting 'horizontally' (Occhiuto 2021) to have a business regulated by a different policy sector, which may also supersede regulation perceived as detrimental to revenue.

Disruptive innovations like Uber are often ambiguous with respect to regulatory authority and established market categories. As a result actors in different horizontal venues (sectoral regulators) can potentially claim that a disruptive innovation falls within their regulatory authority. Moreover, actors in vertical venues (like lawmakers), who are interested in how a disruptive product and service can benefit their constituents and drive economic activity, can supersede a regulatory agency to produce new regulations in line with an entrepreneurial firm's practices. (Occhiuto 2021: 5)

Finally, it is worth noting that effective regulation can be established and enforced. It occasionally, with Uber, has led to the business abandoning, at least temporarily, the jurisdiction (dormancy, in Katic and Hillman's [2023] Corporate Political Activity taxonomy) – but elsewhere it has ended up complying with local rules such as licensing drivers as they have in Germany. And in several cities, as documented by Colomb and Moreira de Souza (2023), and by Cox and Haar (2020), who discuss the case of San Francisco, regulation and enforcement of Airbnb has led to substantial numbers of illegal entire-home short-term lets returning to the housing market.

According to the Barcelona city government the number of illegal STR identified on platforms was cut from 5875 in 2016 to 1714 in June 2018 (Ajuntament de Barcelona, 2018a). A total of 2176 flats were deemed to have returned to longterm occupation by the end of 2020 (La Vanguardia, 2020). The Berlin Senate estimated that 2500 flats were returned to the long-term rental market in 2014–2016 (see also Duso et al., 2020). (Colomb and Moreira de Souza 2023: 13)

Different regulatory approaches make enforcement more or less feasible. Cox and Haar (2020) and Colomb and Moreira de Souza (2023) make clear the type of regulation needed to make enforcement of short-term lettings possible, and that is increasingly being adopted for Airbnb. In short, they highlight the need for mandatory registration of short-term lettings, making platforms accountable for only accepting advertisements and transactions from landlords who are registered, and data disclosure regulations that legally require platforms to send regular files containing all active listings for the jurisdiction (Cox and Haar 2020).

Platform power so far – and the gaps

The literature discussed in this chapter highlights the dynamics of platform politics and identifies the tactics of platform businesses in several contexts since their emergence. Yet certain processes still remain largely hidden, particularly those around the mobilisation by platform businesses of users and allies known as *platform power*. What variation is there in the way that platform power is practised? What work makes corporate mobilisation of users and allies possible and effective, and appear independent? How is platform rhetoric, discussed in this and the previous chapter, combined with platform power? What forms does platform power take? Which platforms participate in which form of platform power? This final section outlines what we know so far, and what these gaps are, before we turn to Chapters 4 and 5, which contribute towards addressing these elements.

The extant literature usefully identifies issues around which mobilisations, conflicts and negotiation have become important; policy ideas which have been tried out; and tactics used by platforms in the contexts of these struggles. Especially important have been strategic repertoires of framing, and mobilisation of users and allies, as identified earlier, which tend to be combined together in a PR campaign. Narratives mobilised range from anti-corporate critiques, to modernisation narratives, to critiques of states and of regulation, propounding the idea of self-regulation or regulation via user reviews, slogans which justify particular political economic tactics, such as 'move fast, break things', 'innovate or die' and 'don't ask permission, ask forgiveness', and populist narratives where customers are presented as voters unconditionally supporting platforms akin to members of a political association (Nyberg and Murray 2023). This rhetorical agenda, introduced in Chapter 2, is collaborative, however, with groups, allies and the public often both the targets for, and the protagonists making, these arguments. Platforms generate narratives, in other words, but they also select, curate, combine and hybridise existing discursive frames, and mobilise the authenticity of other agents, in processes of corporate grassroots lobbying. This is something that is discussed in much more detail in Chapters 2, 4 and 5. These arguments also show how platform power, also known as 'corporate grassroots lobbying', 'astroturfing', 'regulatory hacking' and 'regulatory co-creation', discussed in Chapters 4 and 5, are bundled together with claims towards political legitimacy made by platforms. This wider context of struggle is important for understanding the diverse practices, roles and impacts of mobilisation tactics, yet the business-specific perspective and focus on a limited number of empirical contexts means that authors have been unable to differentiate, contextualise or theorise the corporate grassroots lobbying practices employed by platforms.

A small body of work has discussed these repertoire of platform power and makes some specific claims that are useful both in contextualising the practices historically and identifying what is novel. Two different strands of work exist, the first of which interrogates the practice of platform power as exercised by Airbnb, while the second focuses on tactics across more than one platform, attempting to generalise. Here, as elsewhere, I refer to platform power in terms of the mobilisation of users and allies by platforms, rather than the 'infrastructural power' referred to by Valdez (2023) also discussed by authors such as Lehdonvirta (2022), and Mazur and Serafin (2023), who sometimes use the same phrase.

More work has focused in depth on platform power as it relates to Airbnb than other lean platforms, although even this relies mainly on data in the form of platform produced documents (Van Doorn 2020, Muldoon 2022; although see Stabrowski [2022] who reports on some interview data). Van Doorn emphasises the ambiguity around platform power, much of which derives from a lack of empirical data. He draws together arguments made by platforms; in particular Airbnb's claims to 'democratise' travel, capitalism and tourism revenues, with its PR and organising efforts, to promote something it calls an 'Airbnb Citizen' (see also Muldoon [2022] who usefully traces the origin of the approach). Van Doorn asks: 'Is Airbnb a business engaging in regulatory entrepreneurship by instrumentalizing its user base to fight for its cause, or is it a platform facilitating a grassroots movement that fights for its own cause, which happens to be structurally aligned with Airbnb's cause?' (2020: 1814). He gives the interim answer that it might depend on one's vantage point. The answer underlines that there is little systematic understanding of how these practices work beyond the fragmented examples available from activists, journalists and scholars based on the local contexts they know well, alongside the PR narratives of the companies involved.

Filip Stabrowski (2022) begins to develop this understanding, presenting a fascinating analysis of Airbnb's Host Clubs, the particular form their platform power takes, and the accompanying narrative framing, based on two years of ethnography in New York City. He describes Airbnb's relationship with Host Clubs as a 'combination of freedom and control' (Stabrowski 2022: 14), and documents underlying tensions between hosts and Airbnb, and different kinds of hosts. Home-sharers, usually the public face of campaigns, are often critical of those landlords with multiple listings, which in many contexts are illegal and drive most regulatory efforts as they often represent loss of housing for longer-term residents. Perhaps responding particularly to debates happening around the New York City case, Stabrowski (2022) highlights that Airbnb's use of Host Clubs is not solely a political gambit, but also a space where landlords develop collective identity and learn about how to negotiate issues with their business as well as navigate or evade regulatory efforts.

A few authors discuss platform power tactics across several businesses or sectors. Pollman and Barry (2016), for example, argue that the political and legislative ambitions of platforms, and the tactics to secure the changes they need, are fundamental to the transformations associated with the platform economy. They call the phenomenon 'regulatory entrepreneurship' (close to related concepts of 'disruptive entrepreneurship' [Baron 2018], also 'regulatory hacking' and 'regulatory co-creation'). Regulatory entrepreneurship, common to businesses like Uber, Airbnb, Tesla and DraftKings, involves 'pursuing a line of business in which changing the law is a significant part of the business plan' (Pollman and Barry 2016: 383). Pollman and Barry analyse the factors that foster regulatory entrepreneurship, concluding that 'well-funded, scalable, and highly connected start-up businesses with mass appeal have advantages' (2016: 383). Culpepper and Thelen (2020) extend Pollman and Barry's perspective, arguing that 'platform power' of digital businesses resides in their 'broad control over the terms of access to crucial services on which a wide range of other actors depend' (Culpepper and Thelen 2020: 289, note that the term platform power has been used in a variety of ways by different authors, the interpretation of Culpepper and Thelen being closest to Orla Lynskey's [2017]). In contrast to many historical examples of large companies offering services on which people quickly became dependent, such as the railway or utility companies, however, technology companies such as Amazon, Facebook and Uber 'enjoy a direct, indeed virtually unmediated, link to their users' (Culpepper and Thelen 2020: 294) via apps and user profiles.

Culpepper and Thelen (2020) observe that this connection between users – who they characterise as consumers – and the companies is both key to the relationships of dependency and convenience experienced (habituation), and to the political opportunities afforded by being able to directly contact and potentially mobilise users (politicisation and mobilisation). It allows platform firms to 'portray themselves as promoting the interest of consumers in efficiency, innovation, and choice' (2020: 295). Both Pollman and Barry (2016) and Culpepper and Thelen (2020) note this relationship between the characteristics of contemporary digital businesses and the distinctive tactics that they employ. Culpepper and Thelen (2020), however, only use examples of the mobilisation of the *consumers* of platforms. Their central argument is that when *consumer* identities are 'primed', different priorities are held, as opposed to *citizen* identities, which might be primed, for example, by scandals in the tech sector, leading to the conclusion that to challenge platform power, people must be appealed to as citizens.

There are two problems for this argument. One is that users and allies who are not consumers are regularly mobilised by platform businesses, notable in the examples reviewed in this chapter, and the following chapters: drivers, riders, landlords and grassroots associations of various sorts have all played very similar roles to the customers described in Culpepper and Thelen (2020), who are being 'primed' as entrepreneurs; workers; 'hosts', landlords or property owners; and citizens. The examples of platform businesses mobilising non-consumers are very prevalent, for example, mobilising food delivery couriers to form associations or attend protests (UGT 2021), mobilising ride-hailing companies' drivers to support petitions about proposed regulation, attend demonstrations, or to 'demobilise' drivers using anti-union messaging (various), and mobilising landlords to sign petitions, create associations and personally lobby politicians (see Chapters 4 and 5). Furthermore, one form of platform power, the seeking and mobilisation of third-party allies (see the section on 'Grassroots alliances' in Chapter 4 and Table 4.1), only indirectly target users, through existing third party associations with their own civic legitimacy. The close connection or leverage which platforms have with consumers, according to Culpepper and Thelen, is therefore better characterised as a power deriving from *the logistically strategic position held by platforms in mediating between different types of user* (Srnicek 2016, Valdez 2023).

A second issue with the existing understanding of platform power is that Culpepper and Thelen (2020) somewhat over-state the distinction between a 'consumer' and a 'citizen' identity. Consumption, in contemporary societies, is already regularly framed *as* citizenship, through practices of ethical and sustainable consumption (for example, Barnett et al 2010), and the ambivalent figure of the citizen-consumer (Trentmann 2007, Soper and Trentmann 2008), while citizenship is often, and increasingly, framed *as consumption* in neoliberal societies (Streeck 2012). One could argue that consumer politics, for at least two decades, has already popularly invoked tropes of citizenship, such that the distinction between priming one identity and another might be blurred, with mobilisations appealing to people as citizens and consumers, if they are consumers, at the same time.

A number of further gaps exist in our understandings of platform power which will be addressed in the next two chapters. First, none of the work on the topic to date contextualises it in the history of corporate grassroots lobbying and corporate political activity. Platform power combines new elements common to platforms, especially their relationship with data – that are very well depicted by authors such as Culpepper and Thelen (2020) – with some established practices of 'corporate grassroots lobbying', among other traditions from civil society and marketing, which have tended to be elided in research until now (see Chapter 4). This makes it difficult to see what is innovative about platform power. Second, the literature has, with the exceptions of Culpepper and Thelen (2020) and Pollman and Barry (2016) existed in silos, attached to specific businesses or sectors, usually in specific regions, with the case study model thus hiding common tactics and trajectories. Third, despite a growing empirical base, there is not very much data about the processes that make platform power possible, or the important matter of the precise nature of the relationships between the apparently grassroots initiatives and the businesses. This absence makes it difficult to evaluate the wider meanings of platform power, around, for example: neoliberalism; moral economy; and the blurring of lines between the logics of economy and politics – whether seen in terms of citizenship and consumption – corporate social responsibility and corporate political activity, or commercial profit and democracy.

Zooming out, this chapter has argued that the emerging literature on the political struggles in the platform economy identifies interactions and confrontations that are in some ways specific to contexts and to businesses. Yet in a number of respects, there are some important commonalities, which have not previously been identified by academic work. The commonalities offer the possibility of identifying the lean platform repertoire of contention: a broad set of similar practices, employed in a similar order, across short-term lettings platforms, ride-hailing companies and food delivery companies. Finally, the chapter focused on the concept of platform power as it has been framed in the literature so far, and identifies some problems and gaps. As yet, little is known about how platform power works, the ways in which it innovates on existing repertoires, whether there is variation in the forms that it takes, and its relationships with political economy and democratic norms. This is the subject matter of Chapter 4.

4

The Practices of Platform Power: A Typology

How new is platform power?

This chapter examines how corporate grassroots lobbying (CGL) is employed by lean platforms in *platform power*: the mobilisation of users and allies towards political outcomes by platform corporations. Platform power, it is argued, takes four main forms, each of which combine and innovate around existing practices.[1] CGL has become an important tool for businesses in the new digital economy to shape regulation and influence public opinion, and this chapter seeks to explain its origins and what forms it takes. At the end of the chapter the wider political and economic context in which platform power should be understood, and its wider implications, are described. Here, it is argued that platform power, among other contemporary trends, extends the dynamic in which corporate institutions and logics increasingly dominate political as well as social life. At the same time, it is argued, platform power is simultaneously reactive to, and dependent on, the power and legitimacy of grassroots collective action. Platforms mobilise their users and allies in order to neutralise critical and increasingly successful social movements, but the success of platform power in generating corporate counter-movements has so far been only partial.

Before that, I argue against literature which has suggested that digital platforms have their own entirely distinctive political logics, and that platform power is a new phenomenon (Pollman and Barry 2016, Culpepper and Thelen 2020). Rather, platform power combines new elements with several established practices, especially drawing from the tradition of corporate political organising. These practices have been innovated on in five ways, in particular around platforms' particular connection with their users and their intensive collection of data, and the adoption and further professionalisation of civil society practices such as community organising.

Corporate political mobilisation as a political strategy of firms is mainly practised in North America, and has taken various forms historically (see Walker and Rea 2014). When it involves ordinary people or citizens it is generally referred to using the concept of CGL. Until recently, it relied on the outsourcing of grassroots political action by corporations, trade associations, some advocacy organisations and electoral campaigning to third parties, which became increasingly common in the United States through the development of public affairs consultancies during the 1980s (Walker 2014). The consultancies which do the majority of this work rely mainly on contracts with corporations and political parties. The practices have developed rapidly, in part due to the evolution of new digital methods of collecting and analysing data about political preferences (Howard 2006). The development of core tactics around CGL are charted by Walker (2014), who locates the emergence of public relations (PR) campaigning in relation to politics as particularly important. Early figures such as Edward Bernays set out many of the principles of mobilising alternative voices for political purposes, whether through front groups, experts, or other potential allies and third parties. Also important was the expansion of grassroots interest groups in the 1970s in the United States, which led to significant corporate unease and the coordination of businesses to create their own associations, around reducing support for state regulation, evading consumer protections considered burdensome, decreasing the power of labour unions, shifting taxation burdens, and liberalising market mechanisms (Waterhouse 2013). Mobilising these trade associations, small business owners, corporation employees and customers, and other allies became important in influencing politicians and policy around potential regulation, and both 'grassroots' and traditional lobbying by businesses rapidly increased as these methods enjoyed success in terms of legislative victories (Waterhouse 2013). Most central among industries engaging in CGL have been the food and drink, fossil fuel, pharmaceutical and tobacco industries. To date, little empirical data shows it being used outside of North America, a view confirmed by one interviewee whose background was in international lobbying. Platform power allows platform businesses to deploy some similar practices to the CGL repertoires analysed by these and other authors, but I have identified five ways in which it regularly differs from existing repertoires.

First, in platform power, platforms *collect specific data about their users and often have convenient and unmediated channels for communicating with them.* Important here is the infrastructure of apps, which can target push button notifications and in-app advertising at thousands of users in a particular area, and more generally the strategic filtering of personal data collected routinely in user profiles, more important for Airbnb, which also is commonly used outside of its app format. These data reduce the costs of political engagements, allow the company to maintain control over the nature of the information provided to the potential activist, and make it possible to find and curate grassroots initiatives by cherry-picking certain potential participants or to mobilise particular constituencies. Second, and because of these data, while CGL normally involves persuading existing activists to join a corporate cause around shared aims, platform power *also regularly involves mobilising ordinary people, normally users.* This involves mobilising customers based on perceived dependency on the 'convenience' of their products (Culpepper and Thelen 2020), although workers, landlords and other users have also been successfully targeted. Third, the data-mediated relationship with these users also frequently means that platform economy businesses, in contrast with cases described in the literature, *initiate their own in-house grassroots strategies* rather than, or alongside, PR and public affairs consultancies that have been so pivotal in developing practices of CGL. Fourth, there are *additional influences and traditions* that platform businesses may draw on in their practices of platform power, including, for example, community organising, especially forms adopted in recent years in electoral campaigning, other civil society tactics, and techniques from marketing and customer service such as community management practices (see Table 4.1). Finally, as discussed earlier, these practices hold particular significance due to the nature of platform businesses: *platform businesses often need to proactively campaign for legal change in order simply to exist.* Indeed, Pollman and Barry (2016), as reviewed in Chapter 3, point out that CGL by platform businesses and start-ups is central to the business model, compared with other industries where it is an occasional or defensive approach. It is also worth mentioning that platform power is being applied much more widely, and in a vastly greater number of national contexts, than has been the case for CGL. Platform power is rejuvenating, innovating on and mainstreaming practices from CGL.

In sum, this book takes the position that platform power has a range of distinctive characteristics, which build on existing tactics developed in other industries. These five innovations in the way that platform power is performed, and the variation between the main approaches used by platform businesses, are illustrated in turn in the subsections that follow.

I now turn to identify, on the basis of the empirical material introduced in Chapter 1, the four main approaches to platform power that have been used by lean platforms, with their own distinctive characteristics and particular trajectories of influence from other sectors, most prominently food and drink, tobacco, pharmaceutical and fossil fuel industries (see Table 4.1). The following sections explicate these four forms of platform power, with some distinctive characteristics. These forms are: *temporary mobilisation* of a platform's user base and supporters; the selection and mobilisation of users or supporters via *curated storytelling*, deployed broadly in platform businesses' public policy activities; *front groups* from selected users or allies which may claim to be 'grassroots' and act in the civil society sphere; and *grassroots alliances* with existing civil society

Table 4.1: Mapping variation, innovation and trajectories in platform power

	Temporary mobilisation	Curated storytelling	Front groups	Grassroots alliances
Sectors, companies, examples	**Ride-hailing**: Uber, Lyft; **short-term lets**: Airbnb; **e-scooters**: Bird; **delivery**: Deliveroo, Glovo and Stuart.	**Short-term lets**: Airbnb; **e-scooters**: Bird; **vaping**: JUUL.	**Short-term lets**: Airbnb (for example, Home Sharing Clubs); **ride-hailing**: Uber and Lyft (for example, I'm Independent, Flexible Work for New York **delivery**: Deliveroo and Glovo (for example, AsoRiders, APRA, AAR, RU); cryptocurrency (for example, Stand With Crypto groups); and **platform economy or tech companies working together** (for example, Peers, SF-CITI).	**Short-term lets**: Airbnb; **ride-hailing**: Uber, Lyft, **delivery**: Deliveroo; Glovo and Stuart (for example, Spanish organisations include AsoRiders, APRA, AAR, RU).
Forms taken	Public petitions, mass contact of representatives, mass texting campaigns, many facilitated by apps or user data, demonstrations.	In-person lobbying, email and letter writing, testimony in courts, responses to consultations.	Demonstrations, collective attendance at hearings and public consultations.	Demonstrations, highly mediatised partnerships and joint publications, personal attacks on opposition activists (trade unionists).
Focus and scale	Extensive, unfocused, large numbers targeted, media-oriented, often app-based, short-term, reactive and targeted to moments of pressure.	Very highly focused, participants selected based on specific attributes and 'story'. Stories used in specific campaigns and PR, targeted at legislation or framing threats.	Highly focused, with participants selected based on specific attributes and 'story'. Targeted for specific legislation, but sometimes more proactive. More hands-off than curated stories but not as much as with grassroots alliances.	Targeted at existing organisations and their activists (so more 'grasstops'; see Howard 2006), reactive to particular political and PR threats, usually temporary in nature. Donations normally involved.

(continued)

Table 4.1: Mapping variation, innovation and trajectories in platform power (continued)

	Temporary mobilisation	Curated storytelling	Front groups	Grassroots alliances
Combinations and overlaps with other CGL forms and corporate practices	Overlaps with front groups or grassroots alliances when users and allies are invited to join or support these groups (sometimes with incentives of improved working conditions; for example, see meal delivery companies mobilising for protests against new labour laws, UGT 2021).	Combined with PR, advertising and press strategies. Used in private lobbying. Front groups may also be 'curated', and curated stories may be sought from members of front groups.	• Sometimes front groups originate from user mobilisation (although sometimes there are no ordinary 'grassroots' members at all). • Some front groups become more independent, for example, a few Home Sharing Clubs, several meal delivery company organisations. Relationship becomes one closer to grassroots alliances, and may even become antagonistic to businesses.	Some alliances are with organisations who are very small prior to company involvement – here there are slippages between front groups, temporary mobilisation and grassroots alliances (especially in relation to Home Sharing Clubs and delivery company associations).
History and inspirations	Lobbying by business groups especially since the 1970s (for example, Waterhouse 2013); civil society and social movement activism, especially around e-petitions (see Andrews 2017).	Development agencies and NGOs (Fernandes 2017), corporate strategy (for example, Gill 2011) and social movement storytelling (Polletta 2008).	PR and CGL practices developed in the United States (for example, Walker 2014); tobacco, fossil fuel, pharma and soda (for example, Nestle 2019, Tobacco Tactics 2022).	• PR and CGL practices developed in the United States (for example, Walker 2014). • Tobacco, fossil fuel, pharma and soda (see, for example, Nestle 2019, Tobacco Tactics 2022). • Corporate social responsibility and eco-labelling models.

Table 4.1: Mapping variation, innovation and trajectories in platform power (continued)

	Temporary mobilisation	Curated storytelling	Front groups	Grassroots alliances
Further innovations on and differences with existing CGL practices	• Digital mediation using profile data and sometimes push-button notifications. • More 'ordinary citizens'; fewer existing activists targeted. • Often coordinated in-house.	• Sourced using digital profiles and often via extensive searches emerging from temporary mobilisations. • More 'ordinary citizens'; fewer existing activists targeted. • Often coordinated in-house.	• Use of digital community building practices (see, for example, Giffgaff, as discussed in this chapter). • Both existing activists and 'ordinary citizens' targeted. • For Airbnb, the community organising tradition, and its professionalised versions in political parties, especially Obama campaigns. • Digital mediation used in mobilising for actions organised by grassroots partner. • Often coordinated in-house.	• Often similar to existing CGL practices in mobilising existing activists. • Digital mediation used in mobilising for actions organised by grassroots partners. • Often coordinated in-house.
Debates and controversies	• Transparency: actions appear grassroots-led, tend to be treated as such by media and politicians, yet are initiated by company, and they end when company determines. Business tends to control messaging and goals. • Data legality and ethics: private data deployed is not gathered	• Transparency: individuals appear personally motivated, yet are coordinated and briefed by company. • Selection and exclusion of particular participants and stories to present partial image of users and business. • Input, editing and rehearsal work by elites. • Data legality and ethics (see temporary mobilisation).	• Transparency: groups appear organic and grassroots-led yet are created and coordinated by company. • Selection and exclusion of particular participants and stories to present a certain image. • Some public obfuscation over member recruitment/selection, claims made about membership that are often misleading (Airbnb Citizen 2021). • Data legality and ethics.	• Transparency: grassroots groups appear to be autonomous supporters of business yet are coordinated by company by agreement, who usually initiate partnership. • Risk of groups becoming 'co-opted' and losing their legitimacy through association with business.

(continued)

Table 4.1: Mapping variation, innovation and trajectories in platform power (continued)

	Temporary mobilisation	Curated storytelling	Front groups	Grassroots alliances
	for purposes of mobilising users (for example, GDPR regulations). • Risk of participants being mobilised against their interests (Collier et al 2018). • Possibility of user 'demobilisation'.			• Support for grassroots entities may completely transform them, compromising their independence (for example, food delivery platform associations).
Contextual differences and challenges	• Some concern expressed by interviewees that bombarding officials with corporate-coordinated messages may be counter-productive, especially outside of the United States, so may be less common in Europe.	• Stories are chosen to reflect and represent elements of local context and ameliorate specific concerns.	• Front groups reflect and represent elements of local context to ameliorate local specific concerns. • Greater fear of controversy around CGL, including around perception of greater public sensitivity to mischaracterisation of groups and lack of transparency outside of the United States. In the absence of direct regulatory threat, participants set up more basic networks without physical presence. Similarly, Airbnb's recent 'Community Leader' programme aims to recruit unpaid Host Club coordinators (Airbnb 2023).	• Coalitions made with available partners in local context. • Alliances made to reflect and represent elements of local context and ameliorate local or specific critiques. • Greater fear of public controversy about co-optation or critique of partner grassroots organisation in Europe.

Source: Adapted from Yates (2023)

actors who include users or potential users, through donations, sponsorships and joint campaigns. The categories demonstrate the breadth and diversity of approaches to platform power. They show how and where platforms build upon existing CGL strategies and other corporate and civil society repertoires; sensitise analysis to similarities and differences in tactics between platforms and across contexts; and help identify the key tensions and controversies. Table 4.1 maps out the key similarities, differences, examples, controversies and other characteristics of the four forms described in more detail in the text.

Temporary mobilisation: coordinating short-term and shallow political engagement

The first and most commonly acknowledged form of platform power, and closest to the examples depicted in Culpepper and Thelen (2020), is temporary mobilisation. Temporary mobilisation refers to short-term initiatives where the users of platforms, and occasionally other constituencies, are encouraged to support a corporation in response to a specific regulatory threat or a social movement critiquing the platform. The specific tactical practices include creating and circulating petitions, campaigns to contact political representatives, eliciting mass responses to public consultations, and mobilising for protests.

Many of the practices captured by the concept of temporary mobilisation have been acknowledged in academic literature examining the regulation of platforms (see Chapter 3). The tactic of temporary mobilisation builds on initiatives by tobacco companies to lobby decision-makers and to challenge legislation (Tobacco Tactics 2022); work by trade associations described by Waterhouse (2013) which often asks constituents to target specific politicians in large numbers; and 'grasstops' mobilising techniques where information about specific kinds of voters is collected, analysed and targeted by political consultants, as described by Howard (2006). The key difference is that platform companies collect their own data in the course of their business practices which allows the company (or a third party) to target users through app notifications, email, phone and text message, and this constituency of 'ordinary people' are those who are mobilised, rather than existing activists. Often, as in the examples from Culpepper and Thelen (2020), these are customers, but other users (drivers, couriers and landlords), and sometimes non-users, are also mobilised in these ways.

A few typical examples demonstrate the versatility of the approach and its internal variation. Uber and Lyft both launched temporary mobilisation initiatives in the context of regulatory struggles, most often using petitions and campaigns, in countries as diverse as Denmark, Spain and India (Andrews 2017, Collier et al 2018, Thelen 2018). In London, for example, a corporate petition was created by Uber in November 2017 when their licence to operate was not renewed by Transport for London over a refusal to comply with safety concerns (Andrews 2017). The petition was marketed as an appeal to save the service (#SaveOurUber) and received over 700,000 signatures. Uber also appealed the decision, meaning that it could continue to operate in the interim, and the licence was restored in 2020. In Santa Monica, a criminal complaint made by the City Hall against electric scooter company Bird led to the company modifying its app to encourage users to flood local law-makers with emails (Manjoo 2018).

While petitions or contacting representatives are most common forms of temporary mobilisation, there are examples of other forms of engagement. Spanish trade union UGT (2021) shows how food delivery platforms Deliveroo, Glovo and Stuart mobilised their riders to attend protests against labour laws that the platforms disagreed with. Some of these other forms of temporary mobilisation are also directly incentivised. Over Thanksgiving in 2016 in New York City during a struggle with then-mayor Bill de Blasio, for example, Uber offered $100 credit to students who posted favourable Instagram stories about the business using the hashtag #NYNeedsUber (McKinley 2016) (de Blasio's Uber cap was then defeated, but finally prevailed; see Seidl 2022). Finally, some platform companies have engaged in campaigns which could be understood not as temporary mobilisation, but as *temporary demobilisation*, in that they respond to competing grassroots efforts to organise or unionise (see Walker's [2014] discussion of 'soft repression'). The campaigns around Proposition 22 in 2020/2021, where companies such as Uber, Lyft, Doordash and Instacart sought to exempt gig-economy companies from a new Californian state law which would require companies to grant workers employee status, are an example. During that campaign, Uber drivers were repeatedly sent in-app ads asking them to vote for Proposition 22. Users were prevented from ordering a car without having first confirmed they had read a text message about the laws asking them to vote yes (Murphy 2020). The 'yes' camp spent more than US$200 million on the campaign – the most in any ballot campaign in US history, narrowly winning (Murphy 2020).

The case study of Airbnb helps demonstrate how these initiatives are coordinated, and the degree of work that underpins them. Airbnb also makes appeals to large numbers of property owners in the event of regulatory threats, as shown in Chapter 5, and the following is an example of a mass email sent out to Airbnb landlords in the Barcelona area in 2017 (taken from Iborra 2017).

Hi ___

Catalan hosts welcomed more than 1.65 million guests into their homes last year, but home sharing in this region is at risk. In its recently published urban plan, Barcelona City Hall favors big tourist firms over regular citizens; meanwhile the Catalan government is planning to introduce burdensome restrictions for people that want to share their homes. If this new legislation is passed, home sharing will be considered a professional activity.

The Airbnb community agrees that home sharing needs regulation, but we believe it should be fair and proportionate. Home sharing should not be considered a professional activity, so take a moment and email your elected officials to stand against this legislation and help support home sharing.

Email your politicians

We have seen all over the world that when our community speaks out, lawmakers listen. So email your politicians and defend home sharing today.

Thank you,
The Airbnb Team

Interviewees who had worked for Airbnb in several different national contexts described making repeated contact with landlords along similar lines, asking them to attend certain mobilisations or to call or write to a representative. In these actions, large volumes of landlords were mobilised fairly indiscriminately, whereas for hearings they were very carefully selected (see the sections on 'Curated storytelling' in this chapter and 'Who joins Airbnb's mobilisation initiatives?' in Chapter 5). In temporary mobilisations, platform rhetoric is bolstered and legitimated through the appearance of mass public support, which was compared favourably to traditional lobbying by several interviewees.

The first Airbnb campaigns to adopt temporary mobilisation, based on interviewee testimony and confirmed by secondary accounts, were in Barcelona, San Francisco and New York City, in 2014–2016. Focusing on San Francisco as an example (see Stabrowski [2017, 2022] for the equivalent for New York City) illustrates the first of a series of highly resourced temporary mobilisations, and it was also the moment where one of Airbnb's new grassroots lobbying policies of creating longer-standing front groups (see the section on 'Front groups' in this chapter) was announced. Dwindling stocks of affordable housing in the city had led to campaigners successfully collecting sufficient signatures from residents needed to launch a referendum, 'Proposition F', in 2014, which asked citizens to vote on various measures to stiffen regulations around short-term rentals, including the limiting of listings where the owner is not present to no more than 75 nights per year, in order to restrict numbers of short-term lettings which might be otherwise used for housing. Airbnb's initiative, typical for the CGL examples covered in the literature and these data, emerged as a response to this initial pushback from citizen pressure. Airbnb's campaign cost over US$8.5 million (Alba 2015). It hired consultants, researchers, social media specialists and 11 full-time political campaigners, making 32,000 phone calls to the 6,500 Airbnb landlords in the city, several hundred of whom were persuaded to attend protests and court hearings (Alba 2015). In the press conference immediately following, Airbnb announced that it would be launching 100 Home Sharing Clubs. The emergence of these front groups (see the section on 'Front groups') from a successful campaign of temporary mobilisation illustrates the shared origins of these rather different platform power approaches (see Table 4.1).

Temporary mobilisation also allows platforms to build narrative frames in the context of petitions and text to politicians which can easily be shared with media (see discussion of politicisation, framing and mobilisation in Chapter 3). The control they have over information shared with their users also allows them to 'frame' an issue to their potential advocates before they are mobilised, in ways that maintain fairly close control over the narrative, a level of control which is less reliable for front groups (see the section on 'Front groups'). Returning to the example of Uber's 2017 campaign in London, the petition evoked several themes common to platform rhetoric.

To Sadiq Khan,

TfL and their chairman, the Mayor of London [Sadiq Khan], announced last week that they have decided not to renew Uber's Operator Licence when it expires on 30th September.

By wanting to ban our app from the capital, Transport for London and their chairman the Mayor have given in to a small number of people who want to restrict consumer choice. If this decision stands, it will put more than 40,000 licensed drivers out of work and deprive millions of Londoners of a convenient and affordable form of transport. This decision is affecting the real lives of a huge number of honest and hard-working drivers in London.

The 3.5 million Londoners who rely on Uber to get a safe, reliable and affordable ride around the best city in the world will be astounded by the decision to ban Uber from the capital.

This ban shows the world that London is far from being open and is closed to innovative companies, who bring choice to consumers and work opportunities to those who need them.

Safety is of the highest importance and drivers who use Uber are licensed by Transport for London and have been through the same enhanced background checks as black cab drivers. Our pioneering technology has gone further to enhance safety with every trip tracked and recorded by GPS.

To defend the livelihoods of 40,000 drivers – and the consumer choice of millions of Londoners – sign this petition asking to reverse the decision to ban Uber in London. (Uber London 2017)

Uber's corporate petition describes the app's 'pioneering technology', evoking the trope of innovation, modernity and progress. The petition suggests that political representatives are acting in an undemocratic way, by siding with a 'small number of people' versus 'the consumer choice of millions of Londoners'. By asking app users to sign the petition, Uber combines platform rhetoric and platform power in leveraging the collective interests of Uber app users and ordinary people, while maintaining control over the nature of the political understanding of the issue – provided via the app itself – and the content of the political claim.

Curated storytelling: selecting, editing and rehearsing user 'stories' for lobbying

In contrast to temporary mobilisation, which is broadly targeted, curated storytelling involves the selection and recruitment of particular users whose personal lives become discursive resources in a company's political struggles, presenting or highlighting elements of the business which are not fully representative. Subsequent to the selection of potential participants, there is a process of co-creation of their 'story', a process which is described here using the example of Airbnb.[2]

So far, curated storytelling has not been covered in the platform economy or the wider lobbying or CGL literature, and potentially it is the most difficult to research because it is difficult to see the work underpinning the stories generated. However, the approach can be contextualised in several existing traditions. Corporate use of storytelling for lobbying builds on PR practices to safeguard or improve reputation internally and externally (Gill 2011), and social movement storytelling or framing. The term 'curated storytelling' was coined by development scholar Sujatha Fernandes, who describes how personal stories used in narratives created by states and non-governmental organisations (NGOs) can become rhetorical devices claiming legitimacy based on the authenticity of carefully profiled individuals, while 'amplifying some voices at the expense of others' (Fernandes 2017: 5). Literature on digital influencers reveals similar tensions around the instrumentalising of authenticity, with particular kinds of influencers deliberately favoured by companies, and influencers themselves responding to implicit demands on their online personae (Bishop 2021). The practices have similarities to platforms' strategies around framing and narrative (Slee 2015, Adler 2021, Seidl 2022) but there has been no acknowledgement yet of businesses' collaborations with their users in selecting, co-producing and editing stories used in campaigning. It is also worth noting that platform companies' use of curated storytelling is also distinctive in terms of the companies' ability to find appropriate users through the data that they gather in the course of users setting up profiles or downloading the apps.

Airbnb's approach to curated storytelling began, interviewees claimed, by contacting every Airbnb landlord in a city by phone call, a similar approach to temporary mobilisations. But in curated storytelling, organisers would then invite landlords of a certain profile to a one-on-one meeting, which would ideally progress to their agreement to engage in political participation (in attending court hearings and personal lobbying of legislators, or as members of a front group) or in PR campaigns. When asked what kind of host or what kind of story Airbnb staff were looking for, some implicit criteria appeared to guide the search that were important for creating legitimacy. Interviewees always targeted landlords who were home-sharers, usually living in their property, with a spare room. These landlords were also often representative of cultural practices specific to the area; they were often ethnically diverse; they usually worked as poorly remunerated but socially valued occupations such as artists or musicians; were usually economically vulnerable; were always passionate about the local area; and major life challenges such as bereavements or new disabilities were also common in the stories. These criteria allowed the company to 'frame' users as being eclectic, representative of the city, home-sharers, relying on Airbnb for part of their income, vulnerable to regulation, and to thus portray the company in a positive light in creative and diverse ways, some of which might specifically target existing narratives about the company and its landlords. As presented in Chapter 5, Airbnb public policy staffers tried to curate which landlords became the face of the campaign, and they also curated their stories. In other words, staff reportedly suggested or implied to landlords what elements their individual testimony or 'story' should include and not include.

As Fernandes (2017) notes in her work on the use of stories in development contexts, storytelling is ambivalent because it has the potential, similar to qualitative methods, to render the complexity and fullness of experience. It can be a way to give a voice directly to certain groups who may otherwise be marginalised. Yet when instrumentalised and when the voices are selected by a company with specific PR and public policy goals, as in some of the cases analysed by Fernandes (2017: 5), it is possible that, in her words, 'dominant narratives and devices are given a platform while other voices are silenced'. These ambivalent dynamics were also present in the use of curated storytelling by Airbnb. Platform power combines mobilisation of users – specific mobilised storytellers – with specific platform rhetorical frames, and deploys them in individual lobbying of politicians, court hearings, and in other forms of mobilisation or lobbying.

Front groups: third party activist entities created, resourced and coordinated by companies

Front groups are newly created actors which, with varying credibility, claim grassroots legitimacy, and which play a role that is complementary to platform businesses, remaining influenced or controlled by them to some degree. So far, the use of front groups in platform power has taken two forms: *hollow organisations* which can initiate temporary mobilisations or provide statements supporting, and often crafted by, platform businesses; and *user associations*, which are more resource-intensive and yet may hold greater legitimacy and are likelier to become 'independent' of the company – of which Airbnb's host and Home Sharing Clubs are a prime example (see Chapter 5). The two forms of front groups taken by platform businesses are rather different. Examples of *hollow organisations* include tech lobby associations such as San Francisco Citizens Initiative for Technology and Innovation, founded and sponsored not by citizens but by industry actors (Meronek 2014). Another example was Peers, a 'grassroots organisation to support the sharing economy movement', co-founded by the Airbnb Chief Executive Officer Brian Chesky, former Global Head of Community for Airbnb Doug Atkin, and Natalie Foster, a former Obama campaign organiser (Slee 2015). Peers appeared to attempt to recruit support from some ordinary people to bolster their grassroots credentials, but there was little sense of how these members might shape its direction. *User associations*, meanwhile, remain elite-led but involve the users of platforms. So far, the evidence suggests these are mainly confined to Airbnb and meal delivery platforms in Spain and Germany (UGT 2021 and Table 4.1), while Coinbase's Stand With Crypto groups appear to hold characteristics of user associations and hollow organisations. While front groups in the tradition of CGL are generally 'grasstops' forms of mobilisation, where consultancies use existing contacts with activists to generate 'hollow organisations', platform power may take this form or the more intensive and legitimate 'user associations' form. The phenomenon has not yet been widely discussed in the literature on the platform economy: Culpepper and Thelen's (2020) understanding of platform power as consumers would place it outside their analysis. Yet front groups are already a common tactic in CGL, especially in the United States, and particularly in the areas of tobacco, fossil fuel and pharma (for example, Walker 2014, Tobacco Tactics 2022).

In the case of Airbnb, its front groups appeared to arise out of temporary mobilisation, curated storytelling and sometimes grassroots alliances (see also Table 4.1 for a description of these trajectories). The 'Home Sharing' or 'Host Clubs' that result – of which the company last publicly claimed there are over 400 globally (Airbnb Citizen 2021) and for which there are examples across all seven continents – engage in civil society on behalf of the company in a more sustained way than temporary mobilisation, organising protests, talking to press and attending meetings as civil society representatives in decision-making forums around short-term rentals. There are also some additional important influences in the platform economy approach to front groups, as illustrated in Table 4.1. Airbnb's Host or Home Sharing Clubs, for example, draw on what it calls community organising, by which two traditions are being referenced. The first is a set of community organising practices themselves adapted from earlier traditions by Camp Obama and Organizing for America, widely considered important for the Democrat victories of 2008 and 2012, from which Airbnb hired many former organisers (interview data).[3] Second, there are similarities between Airbnb's approach to community and corporate community building practices, for example those of Giffgaff in the UK, a mobile phone network provider that uses community forums to deal with customer service inquiries (interview with employee of Airbnb subcontractor and internet marketing service Standing on Giants).

The selection of participants for host clubs, as noted in Chapter 5, was not arbitrary or representative of Airbnb landlords. Just as individual stories of landlord activists might be curated, edited and rehearsed with Airbnb staff, landlord activists were also selected for front groups carefully. It was widely noted across a large number of interviewees that landlords with more than one listing, the most controversial and accounting for a majority of listings (globally, 59 per cent are 'professional accommodation offers'; see Adamiak [2022]), are excluded, apparently in order to present a more benign narrative of the company (see Chapter 5).

Grassroots alliances: borrowing and co-opting the legitimacy of existing civil society organisations

The fourth form of platform power is *grassroots alliances*. Here companies, rather than create new front groups, establish public-facing relationships with aligned existing grassroots campaigns or groups which include users or potential users, normally by some form of donation (see examples in Baron 2018, Collier et al 2018, Rosenblat 2018, Thelen 2018). In most cases the businesses are seeking public expressions of support from the grassroots actor, usually focused on proposed legislation.

There has been some acknowledgement in the literature already of this form of platform power, although terms used so far vary, from 'stakeholder mobilisation' (Baron 2018) to 'outsider strategies' (Collier et al 2018) and 'temporary alliances' (Rosenblat 2018). Culpepper and Thelen's (2020) discussion of platform power does not cover it. Grassroots alliances in fact most closely resemble established CGL techniques as described in existing literature, out of the four approaches identified. This is because CGL commonly mobilises existing activists or citizens whose political preferences are known to have been expressed previously, who are more easily accessible by third parties such as PR companies or public affairs consultancies. These activists and, often, civil society groups, usually already have relationships with public affairs professionals, who may struggle to reach 'ordinary' citizens and users. This said, innovative elements are still involved: platforms may coordinate these alliances in-house (Airbnb generally did so) and there is some evidence of the digital mediation of mobilising for action related to grassroots partners, when alliances are combined with temporary mobilisations, as with meal delivery services (see Table 4.1).

An example of grassroots alliances (see also Collier et al 2018, Rosenblat 2018, Thelen 2018, Aguilera et al 2019, among others) was seen during Uber's 2015 legislative struggle in California, where Uber partnered with Mothers Against Drunk Driving (MADD) (Kalanick and Withers 2015, cited in Rosenblat 2018) by offering special promotions to the group and initiating a joint media campaign. Uber's donations to MADD led the group to organise a letter-writing campaign to the California state governor and against legislature which proposed that Uber require commercial insurance (Collier et al 2018). Further examples include pro-platform meal delivery rider groups, which were created with food delivery platform support after an initial series of successful union mobilising and legislative proposals to regularise the forms of employment offered on the platforms (UGT 2021). Participation in the first such pro-platform organisation, AsoRiders (the Spanish Association of Freelance Riders) was incentivised by Deliveroo, which offered members significantly preferential terms and conditions: more hours of work, guaranteed non-penalised (but unpaid) vacations, free uniforms and other improvements (UGT 2021: 14). The organisation signed its constitution in the same office of the lawyers which represent Deliveroo in court, suggesting that the organisation originated as a front group. Several other organisations, also pertaining to other meal delivery platforms Glovo and Stuart, soon followed (UGT 2021: 25–26). Protests organised by these groups were supported by the platform businesses through in-app messages (UGT 2021: 34). These examples reflect slippages between grassroots alliances, front groups and temporary mobilisation (see Table 4.1).

In Airbnb's case, it has repeatedly partnered with the prominent US civil rights organisation the National Association for the Advancement of Coloured People (NAACP), focusing on recruiting ethnic minority hosts using community outreach programmes. This appears to be an approach to, again, combine narrative framing with mobilisation to improve the company's reputation in the context of problems with racial discrimination on the platform (for example, Edelman and Luca 2014) and to respond to analysis linking increasing numbers of Airbnbs to racialised gentrification (for example, Wachsmuth and Weisler 2018). This suggests that partnerships with civil society are a way to react to – and counter – criticism for wider problems in the business. Again, like most examples of platform power being deployed, grassroots alliances are reactive tactics which follow successful mobilisations against the companies or legislative initiatives from governments. Airbnb and the NAACP's alliances involve revenue-sharing agreements where 20 per cent of income made by the company as a result of its newly recruited hosts is donated to local NAACP chapters (for example, Airbnb 2018). While research supports the idea that short-term lettings can increase rent gaps and accelerate racialised gentrification (Wachsmuth and Weisler 2018), an Airbnb spokesperson used the opportunity from one partnership with the Seattle chapter of NAACP to claim, without evidence, that 'people have used Airbnb to prevent gentrification' (Vedantam 2019). Because the most powerful social movements contesting Airbnb have been housing activists, this example demonstrates how important challenging social movement narratives is for corporate grassroots initiatives, which often arise initially as counter-campaigns as a form of 'soft repression' of organic grassroots campaigns (Walker 2014: 194). Commonly, those landlords chosen to advocate for Airbnb in platform power initiatives argued that renting a room or their flat on the platform helped them pay their rent or mortgage and allowed them to remain in their home.

Some implications of platform power

This chapter began by tracing the development and emergence of platform power, and each mode of platform power has its own precursors and additional influences (see Table 4.1). Especially important have been existing traditions of CGL, innovated on in several ways, combined with other practices and ideas. Those additional practices include elements from community organising; NGO-led curated storytelling; the instrumentalisation of authenticity in companies' relationships with influencers; corporate community-building; corporate social responsibility; eco-labelling and social-washing, especially important for grassroots alliances; and e-petitions, used widely in temporary mobilisation.

The constellation of practices and understandings which are combined in platform power can also be understood in the context of contemporary neoliberalism and the contested ways in which social and political life have become commodified and financialised since the 1980s. Platform power is a new facet of corporate political activity where people are mobilised against governments and even often their own interests, entrenching neoliberal dynamics further. At the same time, platform power is nearly always a counter-movement, a reactionary tactic deployed against increasingly critical government, workers and activists. Platform power may entrench and consolidate the advantages of platforms but it is also at once a reminder of the contingency of platform success.

Platform power reveals new dynamics in the changing relationships between companies, states and people, and the shifting nature of democratic and political engagement. Arguments about the compromising of democratic principles have almost as long a history as ideas about democracy themselves; nevertheless, several empirical trends support the argument that the nature of political engagement itself is already transforming. Several trends merit attention. Declines or atrophies in voter turnouts (for example, Kostelka and Blais 2021), alongside some forms of civic participation (for example, Putnam 2000), have been noted in several contexts, despite the varieties of political participation that are being measured expanding dramatically (Van Deth 2001). Globally, levels of trust, especially in government, have declined over time (Dalton 2005), and survey findings around trust and quality of democracy, even defined narrowly, seem to suggest that they are strongly correlated (Dawson and Krakoff 2024). There has been a rise in protest, globally, arguably over several decades (Meyer and Tarrow 1998), but especially in the last 15 years (Brannen et al 2020, Bevins 2023). Perceptions of democracy themselves currently reflect very high levels of discontent (IDEA 2024). These trends, together, reflect complex and widespread crises of political legitimacy, in which critiques of regulation made by platform businesses clearly build on broader unease about governance and democracy.

During the same period of time, the influence of corporations over governments has increased, and the balance of power between them is said to have shifted. Platform politics can be seen as an expression of this dynamic, and part of its continued development. Corporate influence is exercised through the financing of political parties, think tanks, direct lobbying and revolving doors arrangements (for example, Beetham et al 2008). Privatisation tends to reduce the control and accountability that the state, and users, have over infrastructure and basic service provision (for example, Bayliss et al 2021). Investor–state dispute settlements allow investors to challenge democratic decisions where they lead to losses in profit, and even sue national governments (Wellhausen 2016). While the absence of statutory registers in most contexts makes the measurement of lobbying activity difficult, rapid increases in total corporate spending have been noted in the contexts for which data is available.[4] There are several other indicators of the corporate transformation of political systems, governance and logics of governance explored in the literature on contemporary political praxis and political theory about neoliberalism (for example, Barley 2007, Lessig 2011). While corporations have long held significant power politically, it is increasingly widely argued that business and finance are seriously challenging and undermining democratic institutions (for example, Crouch 2004, Wolin 2017) and democratic principles themselves (for example, Brown 2015, Fraser 2015). Platform power seems to be accentuating some of these dynamics. In their approach to influencing government, platforms build on traditional lobbying and the classic repertoires of corporate political activity (Katic and Hillman 2023). In rejuvenating, innovating on and globalising CGL practices, platform power further develops the political repertoire of corporate power.

In such a context, civil society is seen as a particularly poignant site for upholding democracy and collective accountability, an assumption which platform power challenges and inverts. Social movements, civic associations and grassroots politics, the main manifestations of civil society understood as the interface between systems of government and the people, have long been framed as a bedrock of democracy and the essential counterweight to the risks of representation and majoritarian rule, and of corporate power. Social movements, civic associations and grassroots politics, it is widely argued, allow policy and government to hear the needs of populations between elections (for example, Almond and Verba 1963), make essential moral claims on societies through unconventional and often controversial means such as direct action (for example, Thoreau 1993, Graeber 2009), form the basis and locus of the public spheres in collective debate and decision-making over matters of importance (for example, Fraser 2015) and generate new ideas, prophecies, innovations and societal imaginaries (for example, Melucci 1996). As such, civil society carries a powerful legitimacy, as a way of discerning what those without voices think in contrast with the multiple ways through which economic and political elites exercise their dominance, and as a way of collectively speaking and contributing to society. Though it has both long been idealised, it has also played significant roles in the politics of social transformation where the balance of power suggested change was impossible, from the American civil rights movement, to global waves of feminist activism, to the establishing of employment rights and protections. That authenticity and legitimacy is widely regarded as pivotal for social change, Charles Tilly (2004) famously noting that the combination of 'worthiness, unity, numbers, and commitment' in the context of public protest became a combination of historic importance in influencing states. Yet in mobilising people against states to avoid regulation, and in borrowing and co-opting practices from community organising and other civic traditions, platforms are inverting many of these fundamental assumptions about citizen participation, legitimate governance and democracy, instead, arguably, using them to further entrench corporate power.

Platform power does not do this alone. The territory is not entirely uncharted: platforms, as have been described, develop and mainstream a several-decades-old tradition of CGL in the United States. Platform power also augments, complements and is made possible by some other parallel trends. First, there has been a transformation of the nature of social movements themselves through corporate logics (Dauvergne and LeBaron 2014), and the wider dynamic of 'NGO-isation' (for example, Jad 2004), whereby conflictual actors are transformed and depoliticised through processes of professionalisation, bureaucratisation and marketisation, often allied to reductions of spending on public services and the exercise of soft power by external state actors. The second of these trends is the blurring of citizenship and consumption, associated with the privatisation of public services, and in the development of forms of politicised consumption. The *citizen-consumer* (for example, Trentmann 2007, Soper and Trentmann

2008), a figure and mode of subjectivity established by NGOs, states, the private sector and some academics (Barnett et al 2010), is also necessary for the rise of corporate social responsibility (CSR). Together, the concepts suggest that responsibility for global challenges and crises lie with, and can be addressed by, individual consumers (for example, Micheletti 2003) responding to, and incentivising, CSR initiatives (Michelon et al 2020). The third parallel trend to platform power which is challenging assumptions about civil society and corporate power is the increasing use of conflictual themes, philanthropy and social movement framings in the PR and marketing activities of contemporary corporations, in examples such as Dove's 'Real Beauty' campaign, Nike's sponsorship of Colin Kaepernick, Gillette's advertisements about toxic masculinity, Airbnb's Disaster Response initiative and Pepsi's Black Lives Matter-inspired advertising campaign, sometimes referred to as 'cause marketing' (for example, Stole 2008), 'corporate sociopolitical activism' (Bhagwat et al 2020) or 'woke capitalism' (Rhodes 2021).

In paralleling and reflecting these three trends, and borrowing from their cultural repertoire, platform power might be seen as another phenomenon which is intensifying macro-dynamics of neoliberalism. Platform power can be seen as an example of what Wendy Brown (2015: 17) describes as the encroachment of logics of neoliberalism onto political life, 'quietly undoing basic elements of democracy. These elements include vocabularies, principles of justice, political cultures, habits of citizenship, practices of rule, and above all, democratic imaginaries'.

At the same time, platform power is reactive to, and dependent on, the power and legitimacy of grassroots collective action. Platforms mobilise their users and allies in order to neutralise critical and increasingly successful social movements, but the success of these corporate counter-movements has so far been only partial and depends, paradoxically, on the continued trust in, and authenticity of, the social, the non-commodified idea of community and the grassroots. Platform-based CGL simultaneously responds to, exploits and diminishes the legitimacy of civil society, yet it would be unthinkable that it would have any power at all without civil society maintaining its power and aura of legitimacy.

Rethinking platform power

This chapter presents a new typology to illustrate the breadth of tactics encompassed by platform power. It also illustrates the commonalities across lean platform businesses, the influences that platform power from existing civic, customer management and corporate political activity repertoires, and the innovations that platform businesses have made in combining these practices and deploying them in regulatory struggles.

This perspective on platform power builds on Culpepper and Thelen's (2020) discussion of the practices, by highlighting several forms of mobilisation not covered in their analysis, and identifying participants – drivers, riders, host landlords and third-party civil society organisations – that are important to lean platforms' grassroots initiatives, as well as customers. It also connects the ad-hoc descriptions of platform power that are prevalent in all discussions of platform politics, but which have tended to be confined to discussions of individual case studies (one city and a single platform) or comparisons of the same business in several contexts. That work, reviewed and summarised in Chapter 3, highlights the significance of platform power and framing, combined – and often presents them as the tactics which changed the course of the regulatory struggles, with failure frequently presented as a feature of the opposing coalition of critics and their own mobilisation (for example, Thelen 2018, Seidl 2022).

Platform power has some precedents. Skills developed in community organising in the NGO and electoral organising sector; lobbying practices developed, especially in the United States, through public affairs consultancies; newer 'community management' practices used to build brand solidarity and reduce customer service costs; and the longer PR and corporate political activity traditions are all important influences and inspirations for the practices. Platform power must also be contextualised in a wider set of neoliberal trends including the encroachment of corporate logics into social movements and civil society; the blurring of lines between citizenship and consumption; and the adoption of social movement iconography and framing in corporate PR strategies. Platform power, together with other neoliberal trends, is part of the transformation of contemporary democracies, contributing towards a complex crisis of political legitimacy.

Pollman and Barry (2016), Culpepper and Thelen (2020), Stabrowski (2022) and others, therefore, are right to also highlight novelty in the mobilisation practices of platforms. The analysis here has built on their work by identifying the elements which distinguish platform power from other existing practices, most significantly the CGL repertoire that has become increasingly significant in the US context. Those innovations are: the collection and political deployment of user data gathered through profiles and apps; the mobilisation of ordinary users and allies (not just existing activists); the coordination and execution of many CGL initiatives in-house; the use of wider traditions and repertoires described earlier; and the absolute centrality of these practices to the continued existence of lean platforms – which rely on changing the law in order to survive.

A remaining gap in the literature has been that the work on platform politics to date has not systematically investigated the relationships between the lean platforms and activists, or explored how frames and mobilisation are combined except in specific city contexts. The next chapter therefore investigates these themes in terms of the role of the company and the profiles of those mobilised by them, through an in-depth case study of Airbnb Citizen.

5

Manufacturing a Movement: Platform Power at Airbnb

Introducing the Airbnb Citizen

Chapter 2 introduced some of the rhetorical claims made by platform businesses and their allies, and explored the way in which platforms and change are presented in public debates. Chapter 3 reviewed the literature on processes and trajectories of struggle around regulation, showing commonalities across a range of different platforms worldwide, especially in the tactics used by platforms. Analysis of platform regulation regularly notes the combination of rhetorical tactics with the mobilisation of users and allies. Chapter 4 explored the forms through which narratives and mobilisation are combined through users and allies of platform who help platforms pursue political claims beneficial to platforms around regulation and legitimacy, identifying four approaches. This chapter explores the combination of rhetoric and mobilisation, and the different forms of platform power, deployed in the most well-resourced example of platform-based corporate grassroots lobbying in the world to date, Airbnb Citizen.[1]

The chapter has two main sections. First it discusses *the creation of the Airbnb Citizen* – the core ways in which Airbnb displaces itself by claiming to represent a community, while training a carefully constructed community to represent the business. It does this by exploring how prospective landlord activists are selected, and the processes through which they are subsequently recruited, trained and mobilised. It finds that participation in Airbnb's political campaigns and the composition of Home Sharing Clubs is carefully curated, with commercial landlords on the platform, the most controversial and accounting for a majority of listings, excluded, apparently in order to present a more benign impression of the company. These findings contrast with Airbnb's public account of the composition of Airbnb's campaigns, which suggested an organic and highly diverse 'community' movement of Airbnb stakeholders. The findings also illustrate the backstage processes of recruitment, political training, mobilisation and coordination that underpin some of the successes that lean platforms have enjoyed in navigating the regulatory landscape.

The second part of the chapter looks at the activists and mobilisations organised in front groups known as 'Host Clubs' or 'Home Sharing Clubs' (synonymous, generally referred to as Host Clubs hereafter), and enquires about the relationship these activists, campaigns and groups have with the company. Airbnb suggests its Host Clubs are independent of the company; however, the support, resources and influence offered by Airbnb is very extensive. Airbnb former staff describe many forms of support and influence, including protesting alongside landlords; organising many aspects of protests; political education and training; editing and rehearsing of curated 'stories'; and suggesting policy that the company wanted. There are examples of clubs disagreeing with Airbnb or highlighting the problem of business hosts, suggesting tensions between autonomy and control (see also Stabrowski 2022). Yet these examples are often presented by interviewees as failures of the public policy team. The aims of clubs and the desire to remain 'independent' are contradictory priorities which staff struggle to negotiate. Airbnb, as we saw in Chapter 2, claims to be nothing *but* their host 'community', however, for the purposes of legitimising the voices of its apparent allies, it also insists that they are independent of each other. There are several questions at the heart of this around representation: who is speaking for, or on behalf of, whom, with platform power? Is it users speaking for the company, vice versa, or both? Who holds the 'power' in platform power, and can it be subverted or resisted? When platform power invokes 'the community' and 'the people', which community and people are being invoked, and against whom?

Who joins Airbnb's mobilisation initiatives? Recruitment, selection and exclusion

This section explores the question of who becomes a participant in Airbnb Citizen's grassroots lobbying campaigns, and how, explaining the process by which associations and campaigns are initiated, and their boundaries in terms of who is welcome. The question of participation is important because it is one way of understanding the nature of Airbnb's relationship to its citizen mobilisation initiatives; it is also important because it depicts the processes of selecting components for narrative framing processes which legitimise the business in contexts where it is being challenged by housing movements and/or regulatory threats. In looking at the evidence in the case of Airbnb, I also test the company's claim that its front groups, Host Clubs, were made up of a diverse constituency of stakeholders: 'a growing network of hosts, guests, small business owners, and local community leaders' (Airbnb Citizen 2021).

While all interviewees, directly involved in Airbnb's citizen lobbying initiatives, were asked who took part in Host Clubs, they did not mention the participation or recruitment of Airbnb guests, small business owners or local community leaders. Instead, Host Clubs appeared to be composed exclusively of 'hosts', Airbnb's name for its landlords. They were also not open to all landlords, but to a particular subset that were chosen for reflecting a particular portion of Airbnb's business. The key protagonists in campaigns were subsequently selected from this constituency, trust with organisers established, and they were carefully trained, as described in the following subsections.

Searching for the right landlords

Airbnb's approach to the recruitment of potential grassroots activists, while much more restrictive than the frequently asked questions (FAQs) suggested, was thorough and exhaustive, according to former staff. First, Airbnb staff made phone calls to every landlord in a city, or those who had certain characteristics (especially the non-commercial hosts or 'home-sharers'). Organisers would invite landlords of the desired profile to a one-on-one meeting, which would ideally progress to their agreement to engage in various forms of political participation or public relations campaigns. Community Organisers in nearly all cases described actively deterring the participation of landlords who had more than one Airbnb listing, or ran Airbnb businesses, in order to portray one side of Airbnb in a way that would improve the image of the company. Analysts suggest that these landlords who were excluded are those generating the greatest revenue for Airbnb (Cox and Haar 2020, Adamiak 2022).

The question 'Did you recruit people with more than one listing?' thus elicited a range of responses suggesting that multi-listing landlords were deliberately avoided.

My mission was actually to keep them away. (Cassandra, Southern Europe)

I mean not really just because they're the whole reason why the city wants to legislate and by that person buying up a bunch of properties, especially maybe in low-income neighbourhoods where the housing is necessary … I felt uncomfortable with them there. (Frankie, Latin America)

We didn't seek them out and they didn't seek us out. … There was just an understanding that we're not in the same team, but we're going to continue to allow them to rent on our platform. (Annie, West Coast US)

We didn't really want to advocate for those big property management companies, it's definitely something that is a bad look, but we weren't stopping them [using the platform] either ... because no one wants to hear a property manager advocate, no one wants that because it looks bad! (Nic, East Coast US)

So I guess that meant if you did find people who didn't fit that profile you wouldn't follow up with them. (Kati, Central Europe)

So, [laughs] we're not looking for the people who are looking to get AirBnB legalised who have a million apartments, doing it as a business. (Anthony, Midwest US)

The selection of Airbnb landlords is very important for Airbnb's narrative framing of itself not as a business, but as a 'community' of home-sharers. It is also a justification of Airbnb's regulatory goals, even though they appear designed to protect multi-listing hosts, not just home-sharers. Filip Stabrowski quotes an Airbnb attorney and policy advisor addressing a Host Club meeting in New York City:

What [Airbnb] is proposing is that people should be able to share their homes without transforming their residential property into something that needs to be regulated like a commercial property. The analogy I always give people and elected officials in meetings ... is that if you have a stoop sale or a garage sale, it doesn't turn your house into a mall. And if you give piano lessons to kids in your house, it doesn't turn you into Carnegie Hall, you don't all of a sudden have to comply with everything Carnegie Hall does. ... So what we are proposing is that short-term rentals are incidental uses in residential spaces. (Stabrowski 2022: 7)

The public presentation of Airbnb landlords in regulatory struggles, the company realised, relied on this narrative framing – of Airbnb as categorically different from commercial lodgings providers – and locating and mobilising only the landlords who would reflect, and repeat, this reality.

So when you have like local councillors and people out there saying 'Oh Airbnb's terrible', you have these hosts who become the face of campaigns and become the face of the mobilisation movement, going 'No, I'm just Dan from Leith and I just need to make a little bit of income', or 'I got laid off from my job', or 'I have a health problem', and you kind of tease out these people. (Manny, West Europe)

We were looking for demographically diverse stories. We were looking for homosexual men. We were looking for Hispanic women. We were looking for small business owners. We were looking for multigenerational San Franciscan families. We were looking for young university students. (Annie, West Coast US)

Curated storytelling (see Chapter 4) captured the *authenticity* of part of the home-sharing 'community', and reflected and constructed the narrative frames used in that context (see also Stabrowski 2022). Interviewees tended to emphasise a *local, precarious and diverse* population of hosts. That diversity indicated that Airbnb staff were also looking for breadth in the stories, which would hint at a population or 'community' which the combination of stories would together evoke. This creative work, described by Manny as 'teasing out', and involving curating and juxtaposing compelling stories, is important across Airbnb's promotional material, particularly their website, several parts of which present high quality photography and vignettes of such exemplars. It also forms the basis of their arguments or 'frames', which are shown in the literature to be pivotal in regulatory struggles (see Chapter 3).

Finally, there were real risks associated with inviting the 'wrong kind' of landlord, or un-vetted landlords, to meet-ups, consultations and court hearings, as Brianna explained:

One thing that backfired is, so like coming from the political world, the more people I can get somewhere the better, and my first event was in [Brianna's area], and I wanted to make a good first impression in the company, so they wanted 15 people there. I was able to recruit about 200 hosts, and that got really out of hand really quickly because the problem is that 70 per cent of their hatred is at city hall, but 30 per cent is at Airbnb. (Briana, West Coast US)

Several interviewees noted the need to select and manage their landlords carefully, because of the levels of frustration at the company among home-sharing landlords, also directed at landlords with multiple listings. There is also a tension here, between Airbnb speaking as its carefully curated community, and that community speaking as Airbnb – and a problem if they are seen to become indistinguishable, as that would invalidate the legitimacy of the community of activist hosts themselves. Airbnb's email to Catalan landlords presented in Chapter 4 asks landlords to 'take a moment and email your elected officials to stand against this legislation and help support home sharing', but before this, states '[t]he Airbnb community agrees that home sharing needs regulation, but we believe it should be fair and proportionate'. The email is signed off 'The Airbnb Team'. A position already attributed to the community is thus presented to the community, asking them to take action.

The 'three date model' for activist recruitment

Airbnb's public policy staff were looking for a certain kind of diversity among single listing Airbnb landlords (see Chapter 4). Yet even when they were identified, interviewees described significant work usually needing to be done before hosts would willingly mobilise. Community Organisers were often initially assigned a particular area of a city, then presented with a list of names and phone numbers of Airbnb landlords. They trawled through those lists in order to collect information about possible recruits (see Stabrowski [2022] who describes the work of eight full-time employees working in the context of New York City). At this point it was common to arrange to meet with those that fit desired profiles in a 'one-on-one' – a meeting which is commonly used in the tradition of community organising since Saul Alinsky – and present them with a small 'ask' such as signing a petition. This would be the beginning of a 'mobilisation curve', another heuristic commonly used in the profession to depict the recruitment of activists into increasingly significant political roles: calling or writing to a local politician, participating in a protest or being present at public hearings, up to giving statements to the media or giving evidence at public hearings. Airbnb's Community Organisers had numerical goals, or key performance indicators (KPIs), indicating numbers of calls, one-on-one meetings, and turnout figures, one US Community Organiser specifying that he was asked to hit or surpass a goal of 60 calls per day and five one-on-one meetings with hosts per week.

Conversations and recruitment began in an open-ended way with phone calls. The process of recruiting and building Host Clubs followed a particular format of sequenced meetings that increase in terms of intimacy and the political 'asks' made by organisers. This was referred to as the 'three meeting' or 'three date' model.

The first meeting, we would bring them to our office if they were able to and we'd invite them to lunch, and just to get to know each other on a not very intimate level. This is the first, kind of like a first date, basic chit chat. 'Where are you from? Where am I from? How did I get here? Are you from [city] originally? This is what we're going to be doing. I'd love to invite you to this event. It's going to be very social and low key. We're not asking anything of you right now.' ... The next meeting is most likely in their house if they are open to that, or a café near their house, in their neighbourhood. We want them to feel like they're on their turf. This is where we start asking more second, third or fourth date questions. 'What is your relationship with your parents like? What's the hardest thing you've been through? I never asked salaries, but it's like are you happy with your work right now? Can you make ends meet?' (Annie, West Coast US)

You reach out to as many people as possible, you make your first ask, you make your second ask, your third ask, your fifth ask and as you're asking for a certain action, and the first one is really as basic as open the door, 'Let's talk.' The first one can be, 'We will invite you for a drinks event', 'A social networking event', 'We will invite you for a coffee', maybe. (Sarah, Central Europe)

The idea was basically to move people along a curve, a mobilisation curve, that was basically you start engaging them with little things, for example they see or like a post or come to an event or something like that. Then they might become a speaker at an event or something like that and then they write a letter to the politician and then they speak to a local politician and then they basically become a host Community Organiser themselves at one point. (Kati, Central Europe)

These accounts were typical in highlighting a trajectory of recruitment that involved extensive emotional labour in building 'friendships' with certain kinds of landlords, which appeared to smooth the way for the asks made by Airbnb to involve greater and greater political commitment and risk.

The role of the Community Organiser, echoing that of the quintessential 'host' in Airbnb's promotional narratives, constantly blurs lines between political action, intimacy, community and business. Meet-ups and group meetings were sometimes used for the delivery of training sessions or presented speakers from the company. Meetings ranged in their topics, from discussions directly about legislation, to presentations around how to improve an Airbnb landlord's property listing (Stabrowski 2022). The goal was to build a sense of camaraderie in the context of sometimes fierce public debates about legitimacy, as well as mobilise landlords (see Stabrowski [2022] who discusses this slippage in detail in his account of host mobilisation in New York City). Examining the meet-up pages for Host Clubs through the Airbnb Citizen web pages makes it clear that the groups who meet outside of the context of a pressing regulatory struggle are quite varied in their topics, while for defensive campaigns things move much more quickly and do not stray far from their regulatory objectives. In talking about the day-to-day work of being a Community Organiser, Taylor colourfully characterises a typical conversation that might precede a meet-up, and towards the end, highlights its purpose:

'Hey, Mary'. 'Hello, you caught me at such a good time. I've actually got two minutes to chitchat.' 'Perfect! Mary, do you know what's going on about Airbnb?' 'Yes, honey. I'm very aware.' 'So, on a one to ten scale, how involved with this campaign would you like to get?' Ten is actually probably host a social and go to a hearing. I'd say one would just be that you just sign a petition. So very minimal involvement all the way up to tangible hands-on involvement. So Mary agrees to have a social at her apartment. … Then I, as the organiser, before I go to the social I will go ahead and set up what we're going to talk about, probably a presentation and then just have a structure for the evening that way that I can still get as much raw and true information out of these people as possible. (Taylor, East Coast US)

All landlords, and in some cases even multi-listing landlords, would be encouraged to write to their representatives, attend hearings and other events where the volume of complaints, the visibility of bodies in the room, and so on, was more important. But Airbnb cherry-picked the landlords who would get more involved, in order to give the most diverse and favourable impression of single-listing landlords, via the voices of these landlords themselves. Certain Airbnb landlords were thosen by Airbnb staff as the most appropriate spokespeople for higher stakes engagement in politics. Groups were seemingly not all invited to give evidence at city halls or local government hearings. Rather, Community Organisers described choosing certain Airbnb landlords whose stories they felt were the most compelling, by selecting among their records and their database of information, the Voter Activation Network (an electoral campaigning tool that many of Airbnb's US mobilisation wing had used in the context of Camp Obama and Organizing for America). The emphasis in Taylor's account on 'information' reflects the fundamental imbrication of narrative framing and actual mobilisation in Airbnb's platform power initiatives.

In sum, Host Clubs did not draw on the diversity of constituencies that Airbnb suggests compose its grassroots initiatives, but were only landlords, and in fact, as with Airbnb's promotional materials, they were those landlords who had only one listing, and who would portray the company in a favourable light. Airbnb regularly speaks on behalf of its community, and asks its community to speak on behalf of the company. Sometimes it decides what the community is saying or speaks directly on behalf of it, and sometimes it simply decides who in the community should speak: the process is characterised by 'a combination of freedom and control', in Stabrowski's (2022: 14) words. A collection of landlords are selected, creating a 'community' out of authentic voices and stories, allowing Airbnb to define that authenticity, excluding certain voices while promoting others. The process of recruitment to find appropriate speakers was highly energy-intensive. Community Organisers needed to gradually build trust with landlords with appropriate stories, a process which involved regular phone calls and text messages, meetings, and other arrangements, which were described by some interviewees as constituting friendship. Only certain landlords were subsequently called on for the process of dealing with public consultations and court hearings. Recruits were asked to perform increasingly political and labour-intensive roles, with divisions of labour generally defined ahead of time.

The question of which people become grassroots lobbyists, or members of front groups, is important because it highlights how the community or association is constructed and its differences from a traditional grassroots political campaign. Defenders of corporate grassroots lobbying highlight that participants exercise their own agency in becoming involved and the way that they become involved. Though accurate, this argument ignores the extensive search that companies make for certain profiles of individual with the 'right' story, and the exclusion of others or who are not followed up on who would send the 'wrong' message. It also underplays the very direct guidance, co-participation, support and influence that companies hold over the campaigns. The next section explores this support and influence for the case of Airbnb's grassroots initiatives.

How is Airbnb affiliated with its landlord activists? Resources, support and independence

Corporate grassroots lobbying is primarily distinguished from citizen campaigning by activists' relationship with their resources and those taking decisions about coordination. In the case of corporate grassroots lobbying a business resources and controls most decisions, and is often responsible for the campaign existing at all. That relationship between coordinators and campaigners matters because it relates to the perceived authenticity of campaigns, and it is controversial in the case of Airbnb for two reasons. First, media reports that have covered the campaigns, and some interviewees, suggest that law-makers, media sources and the general public are unaware of the backing offered and control exercised by the company. Second, relatedly, Airbnb provides no information publicly about the level and forms of support that it offers grassroots lobbyists, strongly implying that the relationship is unimportant for the activity of the groups. Yet, many claims of interviewees suggested otherwise.

> We made some signs actually, as a team, just to give out to people that wanted to hold them. We had a sign making party once and nobody showed up. Well we had a few people show up but we needed to do more, so we made some signs, they made some signs. So, after the hearing, we had a press conference and we had some people speak and they were holding the signs and all that. (Anthony, Midwest US)

The use of hand-written placards and banners symbolises the authenticity of grassroots activism, an expectation which is subverted when a company's employees have made them. Anthony uses this example to highlight the difficulties in mobilising landlords to commit the time needed for activism in the way that Community Organisers hoped they would. Another excerpt from the interviews presents an example of how Airbnb tried to eliminate the costs of involvement for the landlord activists, in this case to attend significant hearings.

Author: And did you have to charter your own buses [to attend the state capital to protest] or was it just getting people on to Greyhound buses?

Taylor   (East Coast US): Chartered our own buses. They tried to make it as convenient as possible, because it's easy for people to be like, 'Yes, I'll get involved', and then they find out that they've got to spend $12 on the bus. They're like, 'No'. So we have to make sure we pay for that for them.

In its Home Sharing Clubs FAQ page, the fifth question was 'How is Airbnb affiliated with Home Sharing Clubs?' to which the short answer given was 'These Clubs are of the hosts, by the hosts, and for the hosts! Airbnb wants to provide a global platform to make it easy for hosts who share a commitment to making their communities stronger and allow hosts to connect, organize and share' (Airbnb Citizen 2021). This section therefore describes and unpacks the forms of support that are offered by Airbnb to participants, demonstrating that the company's claim that the clubs are independent is inconsistent with the accounts of its public policy ex-employees. It is also contradicted by public statements made by senior Airbnb figures such as Douglas Atkin who described the role of Community Organisers in recorded speeches (see Chapter 1), the job descriptions of public policy staff themselves on professional networking sites, and job advertisements posted by Airbnb, which make clear that clubs benefit from a significant amount of professional political training and coordination.

Host Clubs were also resourced in several concrete ways. Airbnb created the conditions for mobilisation by recruiting and selecting certain landlords, as mentioned earlier, it then trained some of these participants in political advocacy, and then coordinated their mobilisation, often in the context of clubs, strongly shaping when and where members would participate, and with what political content or claims.

Once groups of suitable landlords were chosen and established, a sense of trust and community was generated, and lowering the costs of involvement however possible, Community Organisers provided 'training' or 'education'. This education or training was in political advocacy – how to interact with law-makers, politicians and the media. Interviewees diverged on how specific the guidance issued from the company was. To the degree that this education was general, which some interviewees suggested it was, this hypothetically may have had the indirect consequence of teaching landlords how to engage politically in a way that could be used subsequently, and around other issues, thus empowering these chosen individuals long-term. 'We basically just taught them how government works … it's always about making someone feel like they are empowered to make the right choice for themselves' (Iñigo, West Coast US). However, Brianna's account, more typical among interviewees than that of Iñigo, framed this work not as general education, used to empower landlords to make their own choices, but as training for specific skills needed for the Airbnb campaign around regulation, usually accompanied with the identification of opportunities to practise them and any logistical work needed to make that possible.

Brianna	(West Coast US): Part of it was like educating them on how they talk to city council. That's the thing we were educating them on. We weren't teaching them how to be better hosts.
Author:	Did that involve media training as well, or was it just how to tell their stories? Did you run media training, or how to talk to the press?
Brianna:	With the media training, I would have a spreadsheet with all these hosts' stories, and we'd choose four or five and hand them to the press guys, who would reach out to the hosts and set up the interview.

Airbnb trained, or educated, a selection of its landlords on how to be effective political advocates principally in relation to short-term lettings. The company also identified the key political opportunities related to short-term rental legislation that were calculated to benefit the company: for example, targeting relevant policy makers, and locating dates and times on public hearings on legislature where participation might be possible. Airbnb then mobilised and coordinated landlords around these occasions and institutions. The work also included making regular phone calls asking landlords to do these things or reminding them of their earlier commitments to do so, especially important for hearings and consultations.

Depending on the campaign, the work also involved a range of other practices, some already described, and even involved protesting alongside Airbnb landlords, although one interviewee mentioned that she had committed a faux pas early in her employment around this, having mistakenly worn her Airbnb t-shirt, whereupon: 'I was told to go and get another shirt because they didn't want them to know that people who worked at Airbnb were there' (Brianna, West Coast US). Another example demonstrating the level of economic support backing Airbnb's grassroots lobbying was preparatory training that involved flying in Airbnb public policy staff from other offices to help prepare those giving testimony.

> So we scheduled training before the hearing started. So a lot of times we'll schedule trainings at, like, 7am or 11 o'clock on a Saturday, and we'll have breakfast and bagels, and presentations and everything else you can think of to prepare everyone for what we were going to get. … So we will have a mock-up of the training already ready and prepared, and it's Saturday morning, they're here, we've got breakfast for them and orange juice, and coffee. (Taylor, East Coast US)

Author: You talked a bit about the training of the people who would give their stories. What preparation was involved for the court hearing?

Anonymous participant: We had a run-through. We had other teams actually fly in to come and help us, because we would have done the same thing if any other legislation had come up in their cities as well. So, the New York team, the DC team and some of the Miami team I think, flew in and we had the day before for run-throughs. We had the people who were speaking, just making sure their stories were in order. We had a run of show.

Landlords selected by Airbnb organisers to speak at key hearings were trained and prepared, with several interviewees describing rehearsals for the performance of their stories in advance. The preparation was described as important and challenging because landlords often did not initially agree with each other, or with Airbnb. Most interviewees said home-sharers – those who fitted the profile of the clubs and had only one occasionally-used entire home listing, or one or several spare rooms – were critical of professional or commercial Airbnb landlords, such that many home-sharers supported tougher regulations on them (a finding also borne out in Stabrowski 2022). That meant that Community Organisers had to marshal and coordinate the clubs to support goals which would not harm the business that Airbnb received from multi-listing and entire home landlords and were often, home-sharers recognised, jointly responsible with Airbnb for the local controversy.

> The people who were renting out a single room were like 'I think that people who have more than one listing shouldn't be allowed to do that, I think it should be more for the people with one individual

room in their home where they could be able to make some money but not tonnes of dollars'. (Nic, East Coast US)

It doesn't take a big stretch of the imagination to think that there are times when things don't align, on any level. Maybe the company wants one thing, the vacation rental property manager guys want another thing, the home sharers want another. … You've got all these different actors wanting to pull things in a different direction, and it's trying to fit them all under one roof. (Sam, West Coast US)

The Home Sharing Clubs a lot of times would you know, message in a way that the company didn't like sometimes. I remember one time at a city council meeting a person that the Home Sharing Club brought said something like 'I'm a good host who does everything the right way, by the books, unlike these people who own 15 properties'. (Brianna, West Coast US)

It is important to highlight that the examples like that of Brianna, of things going 'wrong' because of someone the club unexpectedly 'brought', and messaging going askew, highlight examples of autonomy of the landlords and the lack of absolute control that Airbnb held over its campaigns and clubs, even after the careful process of selection and exclusion described earlier. Interviewees remarked frequently that they did not entirely control the groups, and that there was significant scope for them to determine their own agendas. Yet the moments where landlords spoke critically in front of other landlords, or legislators, appeared to be seen as unfortunate. The landlords involved were presented as individually odd people or has having gone astray, and the episodes were interpreted as a failure of public policy, even while interviewees acknowledged the inherent contradictions in their own roles. In that way, Nic described a club that temporarily 'went rogue'; Brianna described one club as having 'gone a bit awol'; while Anthony said, of one club, that they 'flipped' and 'went a little off the deep end', meaning he had to cut connections with them, ending the support and resources from the company. More usually, Brianna said that matters like this were best resolved by telling a line manager, who 'would then either have a higher-up talk to them or she would talk to them'.

Finally, several interviewees mentioned their efforts in suggesting or guiding landlords towards achievable and desirable overall legislative goals for the company, the specific political goals or 'asks' that landlords would make. Airbnb public policy staffers suggested or implied to landlords what legislation they might want to push for, and connectedly, what elements their individual testimony or 'story' should include and not include.

I will say we tried to. ... There was an Airbnb policy obviously, an Airbnb public affairs idea in which direction things should move, for example for [city] we proposed a capped amount of days where people are away out of their own apartments, which I think was 120 or something. (Kati, Central Europe)

So we do our best like in instances where our company's public policy direction doesn't align with what the users want we'll do our best to try and educate or convince or provide as much information to be able to help them align with what we think is best because obviously the people who work for the company, they have spent years and years working in public policy typically in the public policy space so they have an understanding that perhaps most users don't but obviously we also try and understand where the users are coming from to help align the messaging. (Macy, West Coast US)

A lot of people say stupid shit because they don't know the smart shit to say, so you'll just take their story and be like 'Instead of emphasising this, why not emphasise this instead? We think that will be more powerful'. And they'll just go along with it. (Brianna, West Coast US)

In summary, modes of support offered to Host Clubs by the company were numerous. Airbnb, said interviewees, offered political or civic education of landlords, identified political opportunities for club participation, curated or selected user stories, edited them, offered preparation and rehearsal with public policy or public relations staff, created placards, co-participated in protests, chartered buses to transport activists to hearings, and suggested political goals and policy that landlords would fight for. As explored in the previous section, all this was only possible through the trust, community and shared identity created by Community Organisers in Airbnb-organised socials, meet-ups, meals and one-on-one meetings, the recruitment and selection of appropriate profiles, and their original extensive trawl through company databases phone-banking the city's Airbnb landlords. Although clubs had some freedoms – many interviewees remarked on their relative autonomy – the occasions where landlords or clubs developed an alternative perspective to Airbnb were presented as a problem.

Redefining independence

In the light of this information, it might seem surprising that the company and its former staff continued to insist that groups were 'host-led': 'Home Sharing Clubs are independent, host-led local organizations that drive initiatives to better their neighborhoods', read the second FAQ provided by Airbnb when introducing the associations (Airbnb Citizen 2021). The company sometimes neglects altogether to mention its own involvement in creating and supporting the clubs, as in, remarkably, the legally mandatory S1 report produced for potential investors and to register their securities, immediately prior to its initial public offering (IPO) (Airbnb 2020).

Indeed, many interviewees repeated the claim that Host Clubs, and activist landlords, were independent, but it became clear that the term carried a different interpretation to what might have been supposed. Many noted that a goal for Community Organisers was for their projects to *become* independent, that is, 'to exist without Airbnb' (Alice, Western Europe), suggesting that it was an aspiration but that was treated as a definition. Mostly, the term was used to mean that the clubs had *some* autonomy, and nearly all interviewees made it clear that they did not believe Airbnb controlled the groups entirely. One interviewee compared the creation of the clubs to having removed a fence in a neighbourhood that prohibited access to another patch of land: '[I]f you take that fence down it's much more likely that people will start taking over the land and maybe doing gardens, or having a picnic there or something' (Sarah, Central Europe). Community Organisers found the aspiration of independence challenging to negotiate alongside their other goals, which were often around turnout for specific mobilisations. Charity (Central Europe), remarked: 'Okay, so [once] there is a club how do you make sure that they are independent? It's a tricky one. As somebody who works for a company you have KPIs and you have objectives – I think it's contradictory, wanting independence while you're also investing in something specific.' Most interviewees saw the clubs as largely autonomous of the company, and used the word independence, but the evidence for independence, the definition of which means 'not depending on something else for its existence, validity, efficiency, operation … not contingent on or conditioned by anything else' (OED 2024) was thin. Independence was redefined in interviewees' accounts of their work, which seemed to describe numerous ways in which clubs were *not independent*, even while there were also examples of autonomy.

A few Host Clubs had been set up before the global policy for creating these associations had been rolled out, and interviewees sometimes mentioned that examples of these 'organic' clubs still existed. I was curious about how *their* independence was understood. I asked Paolo (Southern Europe) whether these 'organic' clubs, one of which he had mentioned in his interview and characterised as being rather different to the others, also had support from Airbnb.

Author: And with the [pre-existing, 'organic'] club, do they have that access as well to support if they need it?

Paolo: They are independent. This is something that they and us
            agreed, that it's good, but we don't sponsor them and we
            don't support them. It's good that they have their own voice
            and it's good that we – I mean we have always respected
            their voice, but we keep doing so.
Author: Why is it so important that they're independent in that way?
Paolo: We just wanted to be respectful of the host, it's as simple
            as that, we are ready to help. But in the first place some
            time ago we feared when we talked that perhaps an
            external support from Airbnb could undermine the
            power or the legitimacy, they could be blamed by other
            players of being the puppet of Airbnb – I'm giving you
            a caricature – that they wouldn't be independent if we
            were supporting them.
Author: Is there a credibility or legitimacy problem with the newer
            groups because they're not fully independent?
Paolo: I don't mean that. What I mean is that in the specific context
            of [city], when the association was created it was better, we
            thought it was better, it's even better.[2]

The problem with having redefined independence was that Airbnb had
no way of rhetorically distinguishing what was better about organic clubs.
Independence was redefined as clubs holding any degree of autonomy in
relation to the corporations which supported them, and represented an
aspiration that was often in conflict with making sure that Host Clubs
were effective in their role in fighting for regulation that the company
preferred. Senior Airbnb staff were also aware that the support given to
clubs compromised their authenticity or public legitimacy, as made clear in
interviews, as well as anecdotes such as the example of one member of staff
who recounted having been asked to remove her Airbnb t-shirt during a
protest because her boss did not want it to be obvious that she worked for
the company. Community Organisers had to balance contrasting priorities
and navigate conflicting interpretations of language in doing their jobs. An
unintended consequence of Airbnb's practices of platform rhetoric was the
confusion and discomfort felt by the company's own employees.

Tensions in platform power for platform workers

Platform power, and corporate grassroots lobbying of any sort, does not
mean that citizen campaigners are paid to attend protests or are required
to present themselves inaccurately, 'acting' feelings or holding positions
that are a masquerade. But Community Organisers held mixed feelings
about their work, largely because many strongly believed in community

organising and activism as a way to positively affect society, and saw there being contradictions in what they were asked to do. Nic (East Coast US) said that she thought the practices 'put a dampener on the idea of collective organising and collective movements'. Or in Kate's words:

> Airbnb really should not have been able to have a campaign like that. And it kind of raises this question of, if in a campaign, one side has every resource and is all hired guns all the time [trained political campaigners hired as Community Organisers], and then the other side is just random community activists, and then people are out to vote on that, that's not democracy. (Kate, West Coast US)

On the other hand, interviewee Brianna (West Coast US), one of several former Democrat Party campaigners, was equally cynical about electoral politics: 'There was a little bit of astroturfing behind it. [But] from working within [electoral] political organising, there's no "pure" political organising that Airbnb is muddying up with its own money.'

Yet Airbnb appeared to deliberately occupy an ambiguous space between the 'fake grassroots' of 'astroturfing' and traditional civil society, where resources and funding tend to be more explicit, and there is more legitimacy. The impact generated by landlord activists giving their selected, edited testimony, interviewees told me, was usually obvious even in the moment of delivery, yet the specific blend of the user's input and the input from public policy and public relations staff was indecipherable to an outsider. The way that resources were allocated allowed the company to benefit from the legitimacy of civic forms of participation, and from the forums and institutions created by the state for the public to participate in democratic processes. Airbnb's control of landlord activists was never absolute, but the freedom they were afforded was structured in such a way that the company benefited from it. Landlord activists *are* genuine Airbnb landlords with agency, and the economic incentives that they receive from renting their property on the platform do not depend on their political participation – even if they are carefully chosen and their stories are edited by Airbnb staff. But the information that is publicly available, and the public face of mobilisations, hides the complex, highly systematic and, in the case of Airbnb, lavishly resourced role played by the company. For Manny, the controversy revolved precisely around the lack of transparency:

Author: How do politicians and the public treat these campaigns? Do you think they mistake them for organic campaigns?

Manny (West Europe): I absolutely think so. I think if a series of people come together in your city and they've made a home-made banner, they've baked cookies, like, you name it, and they come to a town hall meeting or they show up at city hall. They present themselves as people who (a) are informed and they care about this, issue, and (b) they have these really genuine stories as to why home-sharing should or should not be restricted in their areas.

Airbnb's practice of platform power does allow, indeed it requires, some autonomy, freedom and voice of landlords to be part of the process. This core tension is between authenticity and coordination, between 'grassroots' and 'astroturf', bottom-up and top-down modes of doing political activism. Stories generated by Airbnb from its landlord community still originate from landlords, but their performances in protests, court hearings, private lobbying, media comments and consultations also hide the work underpinning the story and the processes in which it is deployed. Another tension is about representation. Airbnb speaks on behalf of its user 'community', often by deploying examples of stories already collected (curated storytelling), and sometimes it asks landlords or allies to speak on behalf of the company (in temporary mobilisation, front groups and grassroots alliances). The company rarely speaks as itself or in its own voice. This makes distinguishing the relationship between corporate power and its civic initiatives tricky and elusive, what Van Doorn (2020) calls a 'parallax view'. The voices of former Airbnb staff who occupied this interface, responsible for the transmission and coordination of the initiatives, reveal the agency of the business itself, in the form of KPIs, policy suggestions and even in occasionally abandoning groups of landlord-activists.

Rebranding, outsourcing, obfuscating

In March 2021, I published a report covering early findings from this research project (Yates 2021). Airbnb, presented with the findings shortly before publication with an invitation to comment, sent a statement simply reporting 'We announced the creation of Host Clubs at a press conference in 2015. Host Clubs have always worked closely with our teams to advocate on behalf of the Airbnb community and we are incredibly proud of this work'. The company then published a new article in the same 24 hours that the report was released entitled 'Celebrating over five years of Airbnb Host Clubs', that appeared to obliquely challenge some findings of the research, restating claims about the diversity of those who participated in the clubs, highlighting a selection of non-lobbying activities in which clubs had participated, and claiming that clubs were particularly important because of the proportion of hosts who were women (Airbnb 2021). Yet despite their pride in the clubs, over the weeks and months following, the company quietly took down the web pages that described their grassroots lobbying initiatives, retiring the

FAQ list, Airbnb Citizen, and other documents cited in the research. Yet no apparent change in policy was announced. The approach resembled how critiques were handled when Airbnb continued to present illegal listings on its website without permits in San Francisco in 2016 (Cox and Haar 2020): the platform removed the visibility of permits on the website.

Airbnb's website has since been updated with information about an 'Airbnb Community Leaders Programme' (Airbnb 2023). This is an apparently less well-resourced approach (fewer staff in the company now work directly on mobilisation) that seemed initially set up to support the growth of Airbnb Experiences, but since expanded to absorb what Airbnb call 'Host communities' too. Under the Community Leaders Programme, Airbnb users are recruited as 'leaders' who can be trained and supported to co-convene or co-organise meet-ups, to run a Facebook account (normally still controlled by Airbnb staff, with template posts supplied by Airbnb), and to encourage or empower others to participate, sometimes politically. These are all practices that might formerly have been done by Community Organisers, and they appear to remain scaffolded by company templates. As with Host or Home Sharing Clubs, without further investigation the exact relationship between Community Leaders and the company remains obscure. The shift resembles a trend which began earlier, as described by one interviewee:

> We used to do training at Airbnb for leaders, so pre-Covid we would do something in person but often we would turn to online training, so the core thing is to talk about what the responsibilities are. For Airbnb that was running a Facebook page, organising interesting events to which people would come along. (Sophia, West Europe)

There has also been a shift in Airbnb's hiring practices around these roles and job descriptions. While job descriptions of staff until 2021 referred directly to the political nature of the roles, with the most common job description being Community Organiser, but also including Mobilisation Organiser, Mobilisation Consultant, Community Campaign Organiser, Campaign Manager, Director of Community Mobilisation, Community Leader, and Advocacy Associate, Advocacy and Policy Media Manager, and Advocacy Strategist; these jobs, and advertised roles, seem to have changed. It is now much more common, similar to other companies in the platform economy, to see new roles (with duties which sometimes overlap with the former Mobilisation team) using more euphemistic job titles, with positions more recently advertised for Community Manager, Community Engagement Manager, or Community Support. Some of these roles are outsourced to London internet marketing agency Standing on Giants, who say that they work with 'brand-owned online communities' and have hired over 20 Airbnb 'Community' staff in the two years since 2021. In their words: 'In 2022 we were thrilled to extend our partnership with Airbnb as we deployed a dedicated team to manage the Host Club Programme across 7 global territories. This community programme supports volunteer host leaders to run local engagement clubs through a combination of Facebook groups and in-person events' (Standing on Giants 2023).

A member of staff from Standing on Giants, and two 'Community Leaders' for Airbnb Experiences, were also interviewed, towards the end of the research process. These interviewees said that there was not a mobilisation element to their work, suggesting that the other roles of Host Clubs were taking precedence over mobilisation. Yet as Stabrowski (2022) shows, community building and political mobilisation tended to happen simultaneously, and so mobilisation initiatives may still have been supported by directly employed Airbnb staff, who tend to control Facebook groups and provide regular templates of talking points for Host Leaders to work with. In summary, some of the practices Airbnb public policy staff described doing themselves in many interviews are now outsourced to hosts and to third-party organisations. As before, it is unclear how independent the initiatives are, how political the groups are or how successful this approach is politically.

Certainly, overlaps in the claims made about the responsibilities of 'Host Leaders', the job descriptions of new public policy roles, and wider evidence of the activity of the clubs that appear operational suggest continuities in the aims and practices of Airbnb's host community support. The original FAQ document for Home Sharing Clubs described their activity as follows: 'Clubs advocate for fair and clear home sharing regulations in their city, share best practices around hosting and hospitality, organize community service activities, and can serve as a forum to connect those who share a passion for home sharing.' The landing page for the current core community mobilisation initiative, *Lead your local Host Club*, similarly, talks about 'building partnerships through local advocacy', helping hosts to 'learn from each other's best practices and share local knowledge' (Airbnb 2024). This ambiguity over purpose is a long-standing feature of Airbnb's own materials about its corporate grassroots lobbying initiatives. Airbnb's public-facing information has now long seemed to fluctuate between offering public-facing materials surrounding its corporate political activity that has been shown to be misleading, or hiding the policy from view altogether. Existing clubs with links to the Airbnb website, as of 2024, have all been renamed simply to *<Location>* *Host Community*, although in other languages some groups still translate to 'host' or 'home sharing club'.

What characteristics determine the selection of Airbnb Community Leaders? What power do these leaders have, and what level and type of independence do Airbnb corporate grassroots lobbying initiatives maintain from Airbnb? Airbnb chooses the 'community leaders' who volunteer to moderate the Facebook pages, and Airbnb staff appear as the sole admins on the majority of the listed Facebook host groups visited in 2022 and 2023. There remain many questions about the processes through which individuals are selected for corporate grassroots lobbying initiatives, and the degree of autonomy of the company that they have. Both questions are central for the democratic implications of corporate political activity, according to Nyberg and Murray (2023), who in their discussion of the phenomenon point to both the construction of a 'people' designed to legitimate and advance a company's political claims, the articulation of claims on their behalf that do not genuinely represent and in fact restrict or obviate any real participation of the mobilised constituency, and to the lack of any democratic accountability of the company. They support Chan and Kwok's (2021) suggestion that democracies are particularly susceptible to the corporate tactic of 'mobilis[ing] the fictitious voice of the citizens to legitimise its business'.

Until recently, very little was known about platform power. A set of mobilisation and framing practices have been identified as pivotal tactics during regulatory struggles, by a host of journalists and academics, as described in Chapter 3. The range of these, and the main forms platform power takes, were described in Chapter 4. This chapter has described and analyses the main forms of work involved with producing platform power in the case of Airbnb. The findings describe a relationship characterised by heavy support, careful selection of potential activists, but with some signs of autonomy – important not only for Airbnb's defence of their corporate grassroots mobilisation practices, but also for conveying the authenticity of home-sharing to the public, the press and policy makers. Constructing, representing, ventriloquising, mobilising this very specific sub-community of Airbnb landlords is critical to framing tactics, which borrow the 'stories' of a minority of landlords. These landlords are mobilised in various ways to support regulatory goals which do not challenge Airbnb's main source of revenue, which comes from commercial landlords (Cox and Haar 2020, Adamiak 2022). There is some early evidence suggesting a recent change in emphasis or reduced spending on corporate grassroots lobbying by Airbnb, even while there are continuities across current approaches and those discussed by interviewees.

6

The Futures of Platform Politics

Three arguments about platform politics

Platform politics shapes how and to what extent platform businesses are adopted, rejected, reasserted and reimagined in our societies. The key tactics by which platforms pursue their aims, it is argued, are very distinctive, yet they are also multifaceted, bearing their own histories in corporate and civic culture. Important commonalities link platforms and contexts in the use of these tactics – across ride-hailing and short-term lettings platforms there are similarities in their approaches to avoid regulation, for example, and there are many parallels with what we know about other types of platform (Zuboff 2019). Lean platforms practise a common repertoire of contention when seeking to avoid regulation. That means that understanding platform politics can help policy makers, activists and citizens learn about contemporary modes of corporate influence, understand where they came from, and challenge them in the future. This final chapter of the book reflects on these arguments, their implications, contributions to our knowledge, and the areas where further research is needed. It also discusses the possible futures of lean platforms and their approach to governance.

The foundations and inspiration of this book are the growing critiques of digital platforms, discussions of platform regulation and the future of platforms, and the identification of new corporate political tactics. Adding to this work, *Platform Politics* provides the first book-length study of the political struggles shaping digital platforms. It also analyses the conflicts around more than one platform business, allowing for a review of the strategies of lean platforms across several sectors. This reveals the similarities and differences in platform tactics across platforms, emphasising a contentious repertoire of three broad and overlapping moments around incursion, politicisation and enforcement, each made up of several overlapping practices. This is the topic of the first main argument of the book.

While comparisons of particular platform businesses across contexts and cities have been very fruitful, these commonalities across different types of lean platforms suggest that there would be value in comparing their tactics and trajectories further, and at different scales. Future work might explore how far other businesses follow this shared repertoire, and whether there are exceptions or patterns of geographical variation. Another promising area to explore would be the variation in responses by states and communities to similar platform tactics, and patterns in the outcomes. And despite a rapidly expanding literature, we also currently know much less about the approaches of delivery platforms, domestic labour platforms and others, and whether they conform to any of these broad patterns and trajectories.

A key finding of the extant literature on platform politics and regulation is the importance of the tactical approach of platform power, especially when combined with platform rhetoric, in the context of attempts to regulate. The second main focus of the book responds to this, arguing that platform power takes four different forms, that it combines the mobilisation of users and allies with platform rhetoric, and as a phenomenon it is only partially new. A case study of new empirical data was gathered and presented in the book, exploring the platform politics of Airbnb across 14 national contexts, based on accounts from a constituency of former political organisers working for platforms. *Platform power* is a phenomenon referring to lobbying innovations in which platform businesses mobilise their users and allies towards political outcomes. Most writing treats the phenomenon as a new development. Previously, a small number of empirical case studies have reviewed the way that it appears to work in specific locations.

The book adds to these understandings of platform power. One reason why this is important is in assessing the claims that platform businesses make about their mobilisation initiatives, which downplay the roles of staff and the forms of support provided by businesses, leading to misunderstanding among politicians, the media and the public. The book addresses this by investigating the 'backstage' to a set of tactics which have previously been enigmatic. Based on the empirical data gathered, combined with a review of existing sources, the book presents a framework for analysing platform power: a typology of four distinct modes in which platforms are mobilising users and allies, and a summary of the five ways that platform power differs from or innovates on existing forms of corporate political activity. This nuances the impression that platform power is a singular phenomenon, challenges the claim that it is solely about the mobilisation of consumers and consumer identities, and contests the idea that it is new. The book traces the history of the four forms of platform power through corporate grassroots lobbying practices in the United States, community organising, corporate community management, and other civic and corporate practices.

This new perspective identifying the range of practices involved, and their antecedents, should not detract from the finding that platform power appears to be significant, if not pivotal, for many platforms in their struggles against regulation. Platform power represents an important expansion in the contexts where corporate grassroots lobbying is practised, and an equally significant expansion in the profiles and numbers of staff involved, beyond traditional public affairs professionals, to encompass those with electoral and non-governmental organisation (NGO) organising experience. Platform power also seems to represent a rejuvenation of corporate grassroots lobbying that is starting to impact other industries, especially electric scooter platforms, tobacco companies and cryptocurrencies.

There are many important opportunities for further research relating to platform power. While corporate grassroots lobbying has a longer history in the United States, especially with tobacco, food and drink, pharmaceutical, and fossil fuel corporations, platform power brings similar practices into contact with several new industries, national contexts and communities. Interviewees mentioned some of the challenges of reproducing Airbnb's tactics in some European countries, raising interesting questions. How do different political, civic and corporate cultures shape how platform power is received globally? What is the impact of the significant expansion of corporate grassroots lobbying into contexts where lobbying is poorly regulated?

Future studies might also explore the career paths of the new intermediaries involved in executing the platform power tactics: discussions with interviewees made it clear that staff moving from the Democrat Party Obama campaigns from 2008 and 2012 into the first Airbnb mobilisation teams, initially in San Francisco, led to community organising being adopted by the company in its model. Where are platform power practitioners coming from, and where are they going next? Analysis of this might help us understand the legacy and ongoing impact of platform politics in other areas of the economy, and how political and civic repertoires move across domains. Finally, future research might attempt to measure and evaluate the relative success of platform power in relation to different platform tactics.

The book also develops understandings of platform rhetoric, the third main focus of the book. The main argument here, in short, is that platform rhetoric is intimately tied to platform power: platforms derive much of the legitimacy of their claims from users, they curate those voices very carefully, and they make sense of this process by redefining representation and democracy. Extant research on platforms has analysed the language of platforms, and has also explored the strategic 'framing' of platforms in the context of regulatory struggles. These have been important contributions, but they have sometimes missed the wider point that the way that we understand platforms, as societies, shapes all other debates about them, especially around their problems and possible solutions. Knowledge is power. Literature has also treated platforms as generally speaking with one voice, usefully counterposing their narratives with those of activists and states. The perspectives of former insiders show that the reality is at once messier and more targeted. Airbnb is, simultaneously, its spokespeople, its public policy and mobilisation teams, its landlords, and its customers. The power of platform rhetoric comes, in part, from the ability of platforms, often by monopolising data and claiming to speak on behalf of their users, to generate a very precise and targeted set of messages for a city, city-region or national context, that appear authentic, independent of the company, and tell a persuasive story. Platform framing operates at two levels: where surrogates are selected carefully for struggles in particular cities or regions; and at the level of societies, where narratives about the Sharing Economy, state regulation, the future, and redefinitions of key terms such as work, corporations and democracy, also play an important role in maintaining the advantages of platforms over their competitors.

Chapters 4 and 5 are also about *the combining of platform rhetoric with platform power in practice*. The phenomenon of curated storytelling, and the work that underpins the selection of activist landlords in the case of Airbnb, reveal striking ways in which companies can craft messages and messengers to deliver them, by cherry-picking particular profiles of user who will support their corporate goals with authentic and compelling personal narratives, then editing their stories, rehearsing them, and arranging their exhibition to media, politicians, press conferences and court hearings. These voices, it must be remembered, are also the result of actively excluding those who might have detracted from this picture. Platforms speak on behalf of their users and allies, and users and allies are asked to speak on behalf of platforms. This makes distinguishing the relationship between corporate power and its civic initiatives tricky and elusive, and greater transparency essential. The voices of Airbnb former workers who occupied this interface, responsible for the transmission and coordination of the initiatives, reveal the agency of the business itself, in the form of key performance indicators, policy suggestions and even in its occasional abandoning of groups of landlord-activists. In their frustrations, they reveal inherent contradictions in producing 'independent' civic initiatives that simultaneously and tangibly further the company's economic goals.

Corporate power, civil society and corporate grassroots lobbying

If we understand the new digital economy as part of some profound socioeconomic changes around working conditions, accommodation and housing, transportation, delivery, and consumption per se, the book highlights the processes and tactics by which these changes come about, as well as the processes through which platforms and their activity are understood discursively. In particular, this underlines the centrality of civil society, framing and political engagement in mediating such socioeconomic changes, usually on behalf of communities, sometimes on behalf of businesses, and sometimes both at once.

As argued in the final passages of Chapter 4, in mobilising people against states to avoid regulation, and in borrowing and co-opting practices from community organising and other civic traditions, corporate platforms are inverting fundamental assumptions about citizen participation, governance and democracy. To briefly reprise and embellish this argument, social movements, civic associations and grassroots politics carry very significant legitimacy in public and social scientific understandings of liberal political systems, being the fundamental locus of public debate, moral censure, a defence against totalitarian forms of rule and one of the measures of the health of a democratic society. Where corporations are able to benefit from the worthiness of civil society by presenting platform power as independent initiatives, therefore, some urgent challenges are presented. In the context of unregulated lobbying and with the balance of power shifting yet further from states to corporations, it is possible that civil society and social movements could become a very ambivalent force, actively eroding principles of equality and accountability by simply becoming additional lobbying tools for companies. In the event of gradual public loss of trust in them as ways of participating in society and communicating desires for change, they would also lose their power to gather voices and force elites to listen. Interviewees discussed, predicted and were openly troubled by the possibility of platform power further expanding.

[Then] you've a lot of people I worked with at Airbnb who cut their teeth working on political campaigns, and it's just a question of do they want to keep on working on political campaigns? Probably not. Airbnb can only grow so much, government relations can only change so much, so they can either do what I did and move into the private sector, or they can go back to [party] campaigning, or they can go to another company and say 'Hey, you have a similar problem. Why don't I do this thing for you.' ... I think it's going to spread much wider as well. Who knows, maybe in three or four years you're going to have people protesting GDPR [the General Data Protection Regulation] and it turns out that it's Amazon astroturfing or Google astroturfing. ... Anybody that needs favourable regulation and has enough money to hire organisers, I think in the next five to ten years they'll start doing that. (Taylor, East Coast US)

Indeed, subsequent career paths of former members of Airbnb's mobilisation teams suggested demand for their experiences and skills in other businesses, including ride-hailing and delivery companies Uber, Lyft, Doordash, GetAround, Lime, Scoot, Spin, Bird and Lyft Scooters, and Juul, the world's biggest vaping company (Yates 2021). Recent 'Stand with Crypto' groups, seemingly led by cryptocurrency exchange platform Coinbase, are continuing the trend. This suggests further potential growth in the practices developed in Airbnb and other lean platforms.

Table 4.1 summarised how each mode of platform power is associated with slightly different ethical and governance issues. They mainly circulate around transparency, in the absence of lobbying regulations in most of the world, and an absence of regulations which would oblige corporations to also disclose grassroots lobbying (such regulations do exist in the state of Washington, and to a lesser extent California and Canada). Much greater transparency is essential to make sense of the nature of relationships between corporations and their mobilisation initiatives, their activist selection process and modes of support. Also important is the question of data legality and ethics: private data deployed in corporate grassroots lobbying has not been gathered for the purposes of mobilising users, so probably infringes most data protection regulations. There is the risk of participants being exploited, and being mobilised against their interests – for example, there are many cases of union-busting activity where users are mobilised against collective action to improve their working conditions. There is also the risk that companies co-opt or compromise existing or new civil society initiatives when engaging in strategic alliances.

Currently, many practices of platform power breach standards for responsible lobbying practices as set out by leading anti-corruption and open governance NGOs such as Transparency International. These documents warn specifically against 'hidden and informal influence', described as 'activities ... specifically designed to confuse and conceal their true origins and beneficiaries from public decision-makers and any external observers. At the more extreme end, this includes acting through front organisations' (Lobbying Transparency 2015: 7, see also Transparency International Ireland 2015). There are four practical recommendations for governments, or demands which might be put to them by activists, citizens and platform users, which might improve transparency. These are not recommendations for the governance of platforms, but rather, address very specifically the challenges around their corporate grassroots lobbying and exercise of platform power.

The first recommendation would be the creation of statutory lobbying registers that include grassroots lobbying. It is widely recognised as important that corporate political influence over elites needs to be more transparent. Platform power, as a significant expansion of corporate grassroots lobbying practices, makes this case more urgent. I follow campaigners in recommending a statutory (mandatory) register of lobbying, as used in the United States, Germany and several other contexts. In contrast with these contexts, however, it must include a distinct category for funds spent on grassroots lobbying or what is sometimes called 'indirect communication'. It would have a spending threshold or a size of business threshold designed to exclude smaller campaigns; companies would need to reveal their civil society 'clients'; and the register would need to include in-house as well as consultant lobbyists (see also Edward Walker's [2014] conclusions).

The second recommendation is that more resources are allocated for municipal governments to enforce regulation around new businesses. In the case of short-term lettings platforms this means protecting housing stocks from uncontrolled continued expansion of listings, many of which might otherwise be homes. Even where campaigners have raised their concerns, policy makers may feel they have little choice due to low capacity but to adopt regulatory options proposed directly by companies and made specifically for politicians, which may not be in the best interests of their constituents, and would create further and broader governance pressures.

The third recommendation is for a review of the legality and ethics of the political use of platform data: an investigation of the data used for political campaigning that is gathered by platform economy companies in the course of offering services. Airbnb, Uber, Lyft and Juul all rely on their initial access to customer data for their grassroots efforts, data which is provided by users for different purposes. According to interviewees, Airbnb subsequently gathered and recorded data about users' personal lives in the process of 'collecting stories'. The accumulation and use of personal data beyond its initial purposes would usually be a breach of European data regulations, and is widely seen as unethical practice.

Lastly, education, training and campaigns to publicise and problematise corporate grassroots lobbying is needed across civil society to further identify and publicise corporate and public relations strategies that are being used to neutralise genuine citizen participation and social movements, to show the contradictions and risks involved for societies, and to increase the risks of reputational damage for companies that continue to use them.

These recommendations specifically concern the use of platform power, not the wider issue of the regulation of platforms or their governance. More broadly, I follow others in believing that the aim for the future of these digital infrastructures must be public and democratic control and ownership. As a minimum, and as a beginning, calls for legal demands to platforms to routinely submit the data needed to understand their effects, and enforce regulation, are important, and achievable (Cox and Haar 2020).

I now turn, finally, to discuss the potential futures of platforms and platform politics.

Platform possibility

Based on the evolution of Collaborative Consumption to date, and the socioeconomic context the phenomenon is emerging within, we believe certain behaviors and ideas will take hold over the next decade in a significant way: People will have 'reputation bank accounts' alongside their normal bank accounts, and a reputation rating that will literally measure contributions made to various types of collaborative communities. Peer-to-peer marketplaces where people 'sell' their excess capacity (cars, energy, spaces, products, food, and skills) will be viewed as a second source of income. Redistributing and swapping goods will become as second nature as throwing stuff away. Car companies will see themselves in the business of mobility, not in vehicles or in transportation. There will be an explosion in services that enable you to repair, upgrade, and customise owned or secondhand products. Instead of automatically paying with cash for many products and services, we will offer to barter talents, skills, and ideas, and virtual social currencies will have become a normal way to exchange. The consumer preference for handmade or locally produced goods will become the norm. Neighborhood networks such as EveryBlock or NeighborGoods will explode and enable local crowdsourcing between residents on creative and social projects. There will be a whole ecosystem of apps and software for our phones and computers that will enable us to share any kind of product or service. A collaborative and sharing culture will be the culture. (Botsman and Rogers 2010)

Almost 15 years ago, a very particular kind of imaginary about the future of platforms started to become influential. Debates about the platform economy have their own temporality, shifting rapidly between the present, future, putative, conditional, subjunctive – and sometimes, dating rather quickly. Stories of innovation, progress, modernity and disruption appear to embrace change per se, making critique itself seem static, reactive, backward or insular. The very rapid, unregulated expansion of platforms following the financial crisis of 2008, combined with deliberate stalling techniques to slow down state regulatory and legal processes, enhanced this effect. Academics have struggled to evaluate the present or recent past in a sector where, for some years, reliable information about corporate platforms' impacts was almost impossible to obtain due to the refusal by businesses to share raw data. The Sharing Economy, as a concept for something that was only ever hypothetical, borrowing and combining a host of progressive and neoliberal tropes, and implying continuities and potential across a huge variety of phenomena, helped secure an improbable coalition of supporters for platform businesses. Yet while Botsman and Rogers' (2010) predictions, part of the first big wave of Sharing Economy enthusiasm, now read as naïve, they also memorialise core tropes at the heart of platforms' rhetorical tactics to secure favourable socioeconomic environments for unregulated or deregulated exponential expansion. It is therefore a useful time for discussing visions of the platform economy, old and new.

Tech businesses not only monopolise or seek to monopolise their sectors, and information about their own operations; they also, as described in

Chapter 2, attempt to monopolise discussions of the future. Narratives of inevitabilism (Zuboff 2019), so common in platform rhetoric around deregulation, are what Boaventura de Sousa Santos (2004: 10) calls conservative utopias: visions which deny the possibility of other visions or, implicitly, of resistance or struggle of any kind. Futures become performative (Wright 2010). Their monopoly is held in part because of the prevailing ethos of neoliberalism, where most politicians offer few or no visions of a good, or better, society, beyond nostalgia (Tinsley 2021). Tech now tends to dominate the popular imagination (Mager and Katzenbach 2021).

Platform Politics is building on recent work that has discussed and debated future scenarios and tech power in a way that underlines the centrality of political debate, negotiation and struggle. Peter Frase's (2016) *Four Futures* explores scenarios based on extrapolating dynamics around the two trends of increasing automation and environmental crisis, imagining a society that is equal and abundant, another that is highly hierarchical and abundant, a third that is more equal and where scarcity characterises our access to the goods and services we need for a flourishing life, and a fourth that is both hierarchical and where scarcity also prevails. Frase's point is that while automation was long imagined to bring about the end of work, its failure to do so is a poignant reminder that technology does not determine societal outcomes, it merely establishes the parameters of material possibility. We might establish our future collectively.

Similarly, James Muldoon's (2022) *Platform Socialism* closes with a postscript set in 2042, where fictional character, Yasmine, describes a world in which a singular Platform takes care of most everyday economic transactions, entertainment and work. Muldoon describes a familiar, but extrapolated, tension between convenience and control, the infrastructural power described by Valdez (2023). 'It wasn't like people had been forced to use the Platform's many apps. They were just so convenient and well designed.' (Muldoon 2022: 151) Yet there is disquiet felt by Yasmine and others: 'The growing inequality of the platform economy and the precarity that it bred led to mounting pressure for something to be done' (Muldoon 2022: 154–155). Finally, a major scandal leads to mass protests. Muldoon's speculative fictional vignette finishes with the beginning of a reconfiguration of platforms, a nod to the significance of platform rhetoric, and an ironic reflection from the narrator on the performative power of perceived possibilities.

The discourse had shifted and people marched on the streets with signs reading 'Platform Democracy Now!' Yasmine joined the protests and spread the message among her friends, hoping to get as many people out as possible.

Spurred on by the mass movements, global leaders voiced their disgust at the actions of the company and vowed to take action. People demanded more control over how the platforms functioned and wanted to put an end to the exploitative practices of the companies. Plans were rapidly put into action to bring the platforms back under control and for people across the world to reclaim their digital sovereignty.

... As she stood on the train on her way to work, Yasmine surveyed the underinvestment in public infrastructure and the vast inequalities that now pervaded her city. She considered how the city could find new ways of organising the platform economy. The moment felt historic in some way. She thought about how others before her might have imagined her world in 2042 and if this is what they had wanted. She also wondered if others had tried do things differently but had been thwarted – as she might be – by doubts about what was truly possible. (Muldoon 2022: 156–157)

Building on Frase, Muldoon and the trajectories of regulation framed in Chapter 3, several different scenarios of future transformation of platform politics are also imaginable. One, similar to the opening landscape presented in Muldoon's 2042, sees the further encroachment of technology platforms into practices of daily life. This might see more platforms beginning to be contracted and entrusted with public services, healthcare, transit and other key sectors of the economy, leading to increased algorithmic governance (for example, Issar and Aneesh 2022) and the increasing societal power of tech chief executive officers. This might see the further escalation of app-based corporate-resourced activism, with corporate petitions and campaigns against opponents organised by businesses and directed against opposition movements or critical state or legal institutions. Platform power becomes indistinguishable from, and gradually substitutes, civil society as it is currently understood. Grassroots opposition tends to be quickly neutralised via vastly better resourced corporate movements who are able to further exploit user data to generate apparently authentic grassroots movements in favour of their corporate and political goals. There is further borrowing of tactics from community organising and other civil society tactics. These, in turn, also lose their meaning and appeal as vehicles for grassroots campaigns as media and public tend to assume that protest and civic participation is usually orchestrated by actors in a way which makes distinguishing 'genuine' or authentic initiatives time-consuming or impossible. Unregulated artificial intelligence provides an additional set of tools for shaping, impersonating and ventriloquising public opinion, deepening challenges around disinformation (for example, Bontridder and Poullet 2021).

Yet an alternative scenario is one where the politicisation of urban inequalities, the injustices and power imbalances in platform work as it is currently configured, and the creativity and anger of some those affected by the digital economy, continues to snowball, via unions, social movement organisations and other forms of collective agency. Experimentation with the social and solidarity economy even leads to approaches to funding and scaling up of these projects that allow them to coordinate services and collectively provision a 'real' Sharing Economy with a vision of common ownership, more accountable to communities than public or corporate institutions, eventually funded by taxation. Challenges to platform cooperativism in terms of scale and losses are overcome by cities, states, alliances and bilateral agreements, and then new transnational regulatory environments, that prioritise social over economic value, with fiscal and investment policy reducing the incentives to grow at any cost. These changes come about through mass movements, worker associations and platform users, who take their turn to 'disrupt' platform businesses and states through boycotts, community organising, industrial action and shareholder activism. Rhetorical tactics of businesses are quickly and widely recognised as propaganda, and any corporate mobilisation initiatives are identified and sanctioned, reducing their appeal for platform users and platform businesses alike, becoming a risky taboo.

Two other stylised scenarios might be imagined. One would be the possibility of consolidated state regulation, which extends to lobbying law and obliges businesses, even in-house lobbyists, to declare and detail the forms and resources through which they are seeking to influence decision-makers. A final possible world, perhaps the most likely for the near future, is a continued uneven patchwork of struggle and regulatory challenge with no obvious winners, and elements of all three scenarios across different contexts.

The current moment, in historical terms, is one in which the first big wave of challenges to lean platforms produced an unprecedented, and probably unrepeatable, political response in terms of platforms' political tactics. The story of platform politics has been a surprising one. The audacity, speed, lack of transparency and absence of good faith on the part of platform companies towards state regulators startled many policy makers, commentators, opponents and even allies. Despite the success of the repertoire in some contexts, it also highlights the progress that mobilisation of couriers, housing movements, drivers and other associations have been making in politicising platforms, changing the narratives around them, and in some cases helping to establish regulations which have returned housing to residents and secured or improved employment rights. It is important to reiterate that the repertoires of contention employed by platforms are largely consolidation tactics: attempts to respond to challenges because they are threats to the viability of platforms, and genuine opportunities for those affected by their negative externalities, or those whose work is coordinated by lean platform businesses. Both platform rhetoric and platform power lose their purchase, and their effectiveness, when they are better understood. As we become more familiar with platform politics, platforms are becoming more legible and more governable.

The central contributions of this book have described and explained the ways in which such social, political and technological outcomes are shaped by struggles, conflicts and negotiations. Identifying some of the patterns in those struggles, and the tactics deployed by lean platforms, is only part of the answer. We need to know more about trajectories, the strategies of communities and states that have been successful in dealing with the challenges of platforms, and the survival and resistance strategies of those benefiting from the innovations. We still need much more data about what platforms do and their political practices. The patterns of similarity and difference among the various kinds of digital platforms are always shifting, and the nature of the digital itself is complex and changing. Future work will no doubt reveal exceptions to the patterns described here, counter-trends, lean platforms which do not correspond to the categories, and businesses that are not lean platforms which do. My perspective is just one way of making sense of platform politics, a significant area of study for which we will need additional theoretical perspectives, especially around political economy, and a historicised and precise understanding of the evolution of corporate power and neoliberalism. Comparison with other sectors and platforms, newer technologies, and with industries and businesses that came before, will be illuminating. This all said, emphasising trajectories, interactions and contingency, and continuing to explore the ways in which corporate political activity is developing, will remain important priorities for making sense of the digital economy, and establishing the best approaches for societies to shape and govern it.

Notes

Chapter 1

[1] The main data analysed in *Platform Politics* come from an in-depth case study of Airbnb's public policy initiatives, most recently referred to as Airbnb Citizen, alongside an extensive range of secondary examples and documents which help to contextualise the case study in a wider set of political approaches used in the sector. Airbnb Citizen creates and resources platform power or corporate grassroots lobbying (CGL) initiatives, most notably in its groups of lobbyist landlords called Home Sharing Clubs (or sometimes Host Clubs); and initiatives such as Airbnb's 'open homes' disaster relief work (currently conducted as Airbnb.org). For Airbnb Citizen's CGL work the company has hired hundreds of individuals with experience in grassroots organising and election campaigning, generally in the role it calls 'Community Organiser', which form part of the company's public policy team. Hundreds of clubs were established, and while Airbnb appears to have shifted its emphasis towards recruiting 'community leaders' (Airbnb 2023) to coordinate groups of hosts rather than doing that work itself (see also section on 'Rebranding, outsourcing, obfuscating' in Chapter 5), it continues to try and recruit staff to find, select, train and help coordinate these volunteers.

Twenty-one interviewees were recruited, working across 14 different countries, between the years 2013 and 2020, for a duration of between five months and five years. Online, telephone and in-person interviews were conducted between three months and three years after interviewees had left the company only one interviewee being a current employee, and all but one of the interviews were conducted between April 2019 and October 2020. The participants' average age when leaving Airbnb was estimated at 29, the gender distribution was even, and all interviewees were university-educated. Nine participants worked in Europe, the remaining 12 in North America and Latin America, while several interviewees had responsibilities across more than one country. Interviewees held the role of Community Organiser, with front-line responsibility for creating and convening CGL initiatives and coordinating their political actions. More senior public policy staff were also interviewed, several of whom were present in the first campaigns fought by Airbnb, including two national or supranational Heads of Public Policy, with overall responsibility for the company's relationships with several governments. The data therefore present the most extensive repository of information about the corporate grassroots lobbying strategies of platform economy businesses so far. Interview quotations are attributed to pseudonyms, with rough location indicated, in some cases at a high level of geographical abstraction (for example, regions of Europe and the United States) in order to protect interviewees' anonymity and professional reputation, given the sensitive nature of some of the information they shared (although some interviewees wanted to speak 'on record', ethical guidelines made this impossible). Identifying information was deleted from transcripts, correspondence was deleted and original recordings destroyed.

Findings are also informed by additional data analysis of documentary materials gathered between 2017 and 2022, and a review of secondary literature, including academic, grey and journalistic sources, which present further additional examples of platform power. Online documents from Airbnb, with references to mobilisation, organising, associations or clubs, or engagement in political participation, were collected, downloaded and analysed. Public summaries of job roles from employees and websites of Airbnb, Uber, Lyft and Deliveroo were collated. These were used to compare company and employee representations of their public policy approaches. Newspaper reports on regulatory struggles in the platform economy were also collected using Factiva, LexisNexis and Google in the North American and European press in English and Spanish based on keyword searches around terms including company names, alongside substantive concepts such as regulation, law, grassroots, astroturf, social movement and community organising. These presented additional examples of open conflicts, the use of platform power, the contexts in which it was deployed, the businesses involved, and the outcomes. Other academic or grey literature reporting on political conflicts in the platform economy, similar to that reviewed earlier, was also used to build up a more reliable picture of the practices, their application and their impacts.

Qualitative research software was used to manage and interpret interview data alongside the subsidiary documents collected, and core codes and categories were generated inductively. Theoretical memos and integrative diagrams were used to compare claims made, to evaluate the quality of the evidence and to constantly moderate emerging interpretations through systematic comparison with new data (Strauss and Corbin 1998). The main purpose of the Airbnb case study was to explore and describe the practices and processes (see Yin 2011) of platform power. The purpose of gathering secondary materials was complementary, following case study research practices in which multiple sources of evidence, each with their own strengths and weaknesses, are juxtaposed (for example, Gillman 2000, Hammersley and Gomm 2000): to understand better the context in which platform power is deployed and its effects, the profession and typical career trajectories of corporate grassroots lobbyists, to appraise the extent to which platform power had developed beyond Airbnb, and to gather evidence about the likely future of platform power or CGL on other companies and sectors of the economy. Drawing on multiple data sources also helped to test hypotheses and validate or discard emerging conclusions.

Chapter 2

[1] Though they were accompanied with many other overlapping neologisms aiming to characterise the supposed sector, these two began to dominate. 'Sharing economy' soon took over in popularity in the Anglo-Saxon contexts, whereas the linguistic equivalent of 'collaborative' economy tended to be preferred elsewhere, for example, in Spain and Latin America, and for French and German speakers. I understand the terms as broadly equivalent, and will generally refer to the Sharing Economy, following Slee's (2015) cue in choosing to capitalise the term rather than repeatedly using scare quotes, in the context of discussing the concepts and acknowledging their potential discursive power, whereas elsewhere I will use 'platform economy' or the more specific term 'lean platforms', without scare quotes.

[2] In my interviews with former Airbnb public policy staff, whose job descriptions included helping stakeholders to 'understand the benefits of the Sharing Economy', I asked interviewees whether they used the term and, if so, whether they could define it. Like the gig workers interviewed by Ravenelle (2019), most interviewees did not use it, and many were opposed to the use of the concept. Even those who were more positive about the term's connotations defined it in strikingly different ways. This finding supports the

conclusion that the term is, and was, primarily a marketing and public relations device, playing an important role in platform rhetoric.

[3] Uber's press statements, where threatened or restricted, also regularly denounce the regulation itself, or the local state initiating it, as outdated or 'backward' (for example, Husser 2015), as in the case of Portland where the service launched explicitly against the wishes of the Portland Bureau for Transportation, a spokesperson summarising and justifying their decision to keep operating illegally with the statement 'Often regulations fail to keep pace with innovation' (Blumberg 2019). Uber leaks reports showed that insiders were well aware that the platform was simply illegal in some jurisdictions (Butler 2022, Henley and Davies 2022; see also Del Nido 2021).

[4] Airbnb's first full year of profit was 2022 (Lee 2023), Deliveroo's in 2023 (Shiltagh 2024), Uber's in 2023 (Jolly and Wearden 2024), accumulating, together, losses of tens of billions of dollars prior to this.

[5] This followed lobbying from Airbnb and other platform economies from 2014 for the European E-Commerce Directive, a piece of legislation developed in 2000 for the regulation of information platforms that would allow them to republish material without responsibility, to be applied to lean platforms so that they were not accountable for illegal listings (Cox and Haar 2020). These data are necessary for regulating the transformation of long-term housing into short-term lets (Cox and Haar 2020: 67). The E-Commerce Directive has recently been replaced by the Digital Services Act, anticipated to make regulation of lean platforms somewhat easier (Aguilera et al 2025).

Chapter 3

[1] A small additional literature looks at platforms outside the realm of this book's purview, mainly focusing on media platforms (see, for example, Zuboff 2019, Lehdonvirta 2022).

Chapter 4

[1] Some material and passages from this chapter and Chapter 5 are adapted from Yates (2023).

[2] There is evidence to suggest that curated storytelling is used across and beyond the platform economy. Two interviewees independently claimed that it was being used by colleagues doing public policy work for electric scooter companies, which is plausible based on a number of job descriptions of roles publicly advertised since 2020. A non-platform Silicon Valley neighbour to Airbnb, the vaping giant Juul, employs the approach in its 'Juul Action Network' user advocacy scheme (Juul 2024).

[3] Airbnb draws only selectively from the more traditional practices and understandings of community organising in the voluntary sector. That is obvious when comparing the practices to those described by, for example, the UK NGO Community Organisers (2020). Corporate 'grassroots' organising practices, in contrast to community organising, are not directed at 'injustices and inequality'; there is not a commitment to 'challenge vested interests and unjust power'; the practices are not 'inclusive' but deliberately exclude landlords with several properties; and the practices potentially endanger rather than 'uphold public trust and confidence' (Community Organisers 2020).

[4] Spending on lobbying in the United States increased more than three-fold from US$1.45 billion to US$4.11 billion between 1998 and 2023 (Statista 2024), while the 50 top-spending companies in the European Union's Transparency Register in 2022 had already registered 120 million euros by September, compared with 90 million euros in the whole of 2015, suggesting an increase of over a third in less than seven years (Corporate Europe Observatory 2022).

Chapter 5

[1] Until recently Airbnb's public policy initiatives were badged under the name *Airbnb Citizen* (prior to 2016, *Airbnb Action*, Van Doorn 2020), a collective name and website hosting the public-facing information around several corporate grassroots lobbying initiatives, most notably its groups of lobbyist landlords, alongside a selection of corporate social responsibility initiatives such as Airbnb's 'open homes' disaster relief work (now conducted as Airbnb.org [2023]). Airbnb Citizen and the associated Host or Home Sharing Clubs underwent a rebranding exercise in 2021 (see the section on 'Rebranding, outsourcing, obfuscating' in this chapter), with web pages on clubs taken down and gradually replaced with materials referring to a Community Leaders Programme, through 2022, 2023 and 2024. Overlaps in the claims made about the responsibilities of leaders, and social media pages for clubs, suggest continuities.

[2] Paolo also mentioned that Airbnb had been having conversations with the landlords at the time when the club was launched, which while not necessarily contradicting the claim that the club was 'organic' highlights that it would also be misleading to describe them as independent.

References

Aalbers, M. (2016) *Financialization of Housing*. Abingdon: Taylor & Francis.

Adamiak, C. (2022) Current state and development of Airbnb accommodation offer in 167 countries. *Current Issues in Tourism*, 25(19), 3131–3149.

Adler, L (2021) Framing disruption: how a regulatory capture frame legitimized the deregulation of Boston's ride-for-hire industry. *Socio-Economic Review*, 19(4), 1421–1450.

Aguilera, T., Artioli, F. and Colomb, C. (2019) Explaining the diversity of policy responses to platform-mediated short-term rentals in European cities. *Environment and Planning A*, 53(7), 1689–1712.

Aguilera, T., Artioli, F. and Colomb, C. (2025) *Housing under Platform Capitalism: The Contentious Regulation of Short-term Rentals in European Cities*. Oakland: University of California Press.

Airbnb (2018) Airbnb & NAACP launch partnership to recruit hosts in communities of color. Available at: https://news.airbnb.com/airbnb-naacp-launch-partnership-to-recruit-hosts-in-communities-of-color/

Airbnb (2020) Form S-1/A Airbnb, Inc: IPO investment prospectus. Available at: https://sec.report/Document/0001193125–20-306257/

Airbnb (2021) Celebrating over five years of Airbnb Host Clubs. Available at: https://news.airbnb.com/celebrating-over-five-years-of-airbnb-host-clubs/

Airbnb (2024) Lead your local host club. Available at: https://www.airbnb.co.uk/resources/hosting-homes/a/lead-your-local-host-club-293

Airbnb Careers (2022) Public policy intern, EU. Available at: https://careers.airbnb.com/

Airbnb Citizen (2021) Learn more about home sharing clubs (FAQ document). Available at: https://www.airbnbcitizen.com/clubs/faq

Airbnb.org (2023) Responding in times of crisis. Available at: https://airbnb.org/

Alba, D. (2015) After victory, Airbnb compares its influence to the NRA's. *Wired*, 7 August. Available at: https://www.wired.com/2015/11/after-victory-airbnb-compares-its-influence-to-the-nras/

Almond, G.A. and Verba, S. (1963) *The Civic Culture: Political Attitudes and Democracy in Five Nations*. New York: SAGE.

Andrews, S. (2017) Uber and the corporate capture of e-petitions. *Red Pepper.* Available at: https://www.redpepper.org.uk/uber-and-the-corporate-capture-of-e-petitions/

Arias-Sans, A. and Quaglieri, A. (2016) Unravelling Airbnb: perspectives from Barcelona. In A.P. Russo and G. Richards (eds), *Reinventing the Local in Tourism.* Bristol: Channel View Publications, pp 209–228.

Atkin, D. (2014) Lessons in building movements through community action from Douglas Atkin, global director of community at Airbnb – CMX summit 2014 [video]. Available at: https://www.youtube.com/watch?v=X-PN5WWytgo

Bardhi, F. and Eckhardt, G.M. (2012) Access-based consumption: the case of car sharing. *Journal of Consumer Research*, 39(4), 881–898.

Barley, S.R. (2007) Corporations, democracy, and the public good. *Journal of Management Inquiry*, 16(3), 201–215.

Barnett, C., Cloke, P., Clarke, N. and Malpass, A. (2010) *Globalizing Responsibilities: The Political Rationalities of Ethical Consumption.* Oxford: Wiley-Blackwell.

Baron, D. (2018) Disruptive entrepreneurship and dual purpose strategies: the case of Uber. *Strategy Science*, 3(2), 439–462.

Bastani, A. (2019). *Fully Automated Luxury Communism.* London: Verso Books.

Baum, A. (2018) Resisting the gig economy: the emergence of cooperative food delivery platforms. *OpenDemocracy*, 22 March. Available at: https://www.opendemocracy.net/neweconomics/resisting-gig-economy-emergence-cooperative-food-delivery-platforms/

Bayliss, K., Mattioli, G. and Steinberger, J. (2021) Inequality, poverty and the privatization of essential services. *Competition & Change*, 25(3–4), 478–500.

Beetham, D., Kearton, I., Bracking, S. and Weir, S. (2008) *International IDEA Handbook on Democracy Assessment.* Available at: https://repository.essex.ac.uk/7898/1/Assessing-the-Quality-of-Democracy-A-Practical-Guide-PDF-format.pdf

Benli-Trichet, M.C. and Kübler, D. (2022) The political origins of platform economy regulations. *Policy & Internet*, 14(4), 736–754.

Bevins, V. (2023) *If We Burn: The Mass Protest Decade and the Missing Revolution.* London: Hachette UK.

Bhagwat, Y., Warren, N.L., Beck, J.T. and Watson IV, G.F. (2020) Corporate sociopolitical activism and firm value. *Journal of Marketing*, 84(5), 1–21.

Bishop, S. (2021) Influencer management tools: algorithmic cultures, brand safety, and bias. *Social Media + Society*, 7(1), 1–13.

Blumberg, N. (2019) Inside Uber's dramatic rise – and its CEO's fall. *wttw news*, 17 December. Available at: https://news.wttw.com/2019/12/17/inside-ubers-dramatic-rise-and-its-ceos-fall

Boewe, J. and Schulten, J. (2020) Amazon strikes in Europe: seven years of industrial action, challenges and strategies. In J. Alimahomed-Wilson and E. Reese (eds), *The Cost of Free Shipping: Amazon in the Global Economy*. London: Pluto Press, pp 209–224.

Bontridder, N. and Poullet, Y. (2021) The role of artificial intelligence in disinformation. *Data & Policy*, 3, e32.

Botsman, R. and Rogers, R. (2010) *What's Mine is Yours: The Rise of Collaborative Consumption*. New York: HarperCollins.

Brannen, S., Haig, C. and Schmidt, K. (2020) *The Age of Mass Protests*. CSIS report. Available at: https://www.csis.org/analysis/age-mass-prote sts-understanding-escalating-global-trend

Bratton, B.H. (2016) *The Stack: On Software and Sovereignty*. Cambridge, MA: MIT Press.

Brown, W. (2015) *Undoing the Demos: Neoliberalism's Stealth Revolution*. Cambridge, MA: MIT Press.

Butler, B. (2022) The Uber files: firm knew it launched illegally in Australia, then leaned on governments to change the law. *The Guardian*, 15 July. Available at: https://www.theguardian.com/news/2022/jul/15/the-uber-files-australia-launched-operated-illegally-document-leak

Butler, S. (2017) Deliveroo accused of 'creating vocabulary' to avoid calling couriers employees. *The Guardian*, 5 April. Available at: https://www.the guardian.com/business/2017/apr/05/deliveroo-couriers-employees-managers

Calo, R. and Rosenblat, A. (2017) The taking economy: Uber, information, and power. *Columbia Law Review*, 117(6), 1623–1690.

Cant, C. (2019) *Riding for Deliveroo: Resistance in the New Economy*. Hoboken: John Wiley & Sons.

Carville, O. (2021) Airbnb is spending millions of dollars to make nightmares go away. *Bloomberg News*, 15 June. Available at: https://www.bloomberg. com/news/features/2021-06-15/airbnb-spends-millions-making-nightma res-at-live-anywhere-rentals-go-away

Chan, N.K. and Kwok, C. (2021) Guerilla capitalism and the platform economy: governing Uber in China, Taiwan, and Hong Kong. *Information, Communication & Society*, 24(6), 780–796.

Chesky, B. (2014) Fireside chat with Brian Chesky (Airbnb). Keynote address at *TechCrunch Disrupt SF 2014*. Available at: https://techcrunch. com/unified-video/fireside-chat-with-brian-chesky-airbnb-moderated-by-ryan-lawler/

Cini, L. (2023) Resisting algorithmic control: understanding the rise and variety of platform worker mobilisations. *New Technology, Work and Employment*, 38(1), 125–144.

Cini, L., Maccarrone, V. and Tassinari, A. (2022) With or without u(nions)? Understanding the diversity of gig workers' organizing practices in Italy and the UK. *European Journal of Industrial Relations*, 28(3), 341–362.

Cioffi, J.W., Kenney, M.F. and Zysman, J. (2022) Platform power and regulatory politics: Polanyi for the twenty-first century. *New Political Economy*, 27(5), 820–836. https://doi.org/10.1080/13563467.2022.2027355

Cócola-Gant, A. (2016) Holiday rentals: the new gentrification battlefront. *Sociological Research Online*, 21(3), 112–120.

Cócola-Gant, A. and Gago, A. (2021) Airbnb, buy-to-let investment and tourism-driven displacement. *Environment and Planning A: Economy and Space*, 53(7), 1671–1688.

Collier, R.B., Dubal, V.B. and Carter, C.L. (2018) Disrupting regulation, regulating disruption: the politics of Uber in the United States. *American Political Science Association*, 16(4), 919–937.

Colomb, C. and Moreira de Souza, T. (2021) *Regulating Short-Term Rentals*. London: Property Research Trust.

Colomb, C. and Moreira de Souza, T. (2023) Illegal short-term rentals, regulatory enforcement and informal practices in the age of digital platforms. *European Urban and Regional Studies*, 09697764231155386.

Community Organisers (2020) *Community Organising Compared*. Available at: https://www.corganisers.org.uk/what-is-community-organising/the-book/

Conill, J., Castells, M., Cardenas, A. and Servon, L. (2012) Beyond the crisis: the emergence of alternative economic practices. In M. Castells, J. Caraça and G. Cardoso (eds), *Aftermath: The Cultures of the Economic Crisis*. Oxford: Oxford University Press, pp 210–250.

Corporate Europe Observatory (2018) UnFairbnb. *Corporate Europe Observatory*, 2 May. Available at: https://corporateeurope.org/power-lobbies/2018/05/unfairbnb

Corporate Europe Observatory (2022) A ranking of lobbying activities: who spends most? *Corporate Europe Observatory*, 20 September. Available at: https://corporateeurope.org/en/2022/09/ranking-lobbying-activities-who-spends-most

Cox, M. and Haar, K. (2020) *Platform Failures*. Study commissioned by members of the IMCO committee of the GUE/NGL group in the European Parliament. Available at: https://left.eu/content/uploads/2020/12/Platform-Failures-FINAL-VERSION

Crouch, C. (2004) *Post-democracy*. Cambridge: Polity.

Culpepper, P.D. and Thelen, K. (2020) Are we all Amazon primed? Consumers and the politics of platform power. *Comparative Political Studies*, 53(2), 288–318.

Dalton, R.J. (2005) The social transformation of trust in government. *International Review of Sociology*, 15(1), 133–154.

Dauvergne, P. and LeBaron, G. (2014) *Protest Inc.: The Corporatization of Activism*. Hoboken: John Wiley & Sons.

Davies, H., Goodley, S., Lawrence, F., Lewis, P. and O'Carroll, L. (2022) Uber broke laws, duped police and secretly lobbied governments, leak reveals. *The Guardian*, 11 July. Available at: https://www.theguardian.com/news/2022/jul/10/uber-files-leak-reveals-global-lobbying-campaign

Dawson, A. and Krakoff, I.L. (2024) Political trust and democracy: the critical citizens thesis re-examined. *Democratization*, 31(1), 90–112.

De Grave, A. (2016) So long, collaborative economy! *Ouishare*, 22 June. Available at: https://www.ouishare.net/article/so-long-collaborative-economy

Del Nido, J.M. (2021) *Taxis vs. Uber: Courts, Markets, and Technology in Buenos Aires*. Redwood City: Stanford University Press.

Dwoskin, E. (2017) How a former Clinton aid is rewriting Silicon Valley's political playbook. *The Washington Post*, 27 January. Available at: https://www.washingtonpost.com/business/economy/how-a-former-clinton-aide-is-rewriting-silicon-valleys-political-playbook/2017/01/24/211c4d10-d697-11e6-9f9f-5cdb4b7f8dd7_story.html

Edelman, B.G. and Luca, M. (2014) Digital discrimination: the case of Airbnb. *Harvard Business School NOM Unit Working Paper*, 14–054.

European Commission (2016) *A European Agenda for the Collaborative Economy*. Brussels. Available at: https://eur-lex.europa.eu/legal-content/EN/TXT/?uri=COM%3A2016%3A356%3AFIN

European Parliament (2024) Platform work: first green light to new EU rules on employment status. Press release, 19 March. Available at: https://www.europarl.europa.eu/news/en/press-room/20240318IPR19420/platform-work-first-green-light-to-new-eu-rules-on-employment-status

Fernandes, S. (2017) *Curated Stories*. Oxford: Oxford University Press.

Fernández-Trujillo Moares, F., Betancor Nuez, G., and Martinez Lucio, M. (2023) Guest editorial: debates on social movements and trade unionism in Europe. *New Forms of Interaction and Transformative Identities in Work and Society. Employee Relations: The International Journal*, 45(4), 797–807.

Fleischer, V. (2010) Regulatory arbitrage. *Texas Law Review*, 89, 227–290.

Frase, P. (2016) *Four Futures: Life after Capitalism*. London: Verso Books.

Fraser, N. (2015) Legitimation crisis? On the political contradictions of financialized capitalism. *Critical Historical Studies*, 2(2), 157–189.

Gill, R. (2011) An integrative review of storytelling. *PRism*, 8(1), 1–16.

Gillman, B. (2000) *Case Study Research Methods*. New York: Continuum.

Graeber, D. (2009) *Direct Action: An Ethnography*. Chico: AK Press.

Hammersley, M. and Gomm, R. (2000) Introduction. In R. Gomm, M. Hammersley and P. Foster (eds), *Case Study Method: Key Issues, Key Texts*. London: SAGE, pp 1–16.

Helmond, A. (2015). The platformization of the web: making web data platform ready. *Social Media + Society*, 1(2), 1–11.

Henley, J. and Davies, H. (2022) Emmanuel Macron secretly aided Uber lobbying drive in France, leak reveals. *The Guardian*, 10 July. Available at: https://www.theguardian.com/news/2022/jul/10/emmanuel-mac ron-secretly-aided-uber-lobbying-drive-france-leak-reveals

Hiltzik, M. (2020) How millions from Uber and Lyft are funding the harassment of a critic. *Los Angeles Times*, 2 September. Available at: https:// www.latimes.com/business/story/2020-09-02/uber-lyft-veena-dubal-twitter-bullying

Hoffman, R. and Yeh, C. (2018) *Blitzscaling: The Lightning-fast Path to Building Massively Valuable Companies*. New York: HarperCollins.

Howard, P.N. (2006) *New Media Campaigns and the Managed Citizen*. Cambridge: Cambridge University Press.

Husser, A. (2015) Taxis likely hurting themselves, helping Uber with protests. *CBC News*, 13 December. Available at: https://www.cbc.ca/news/business/ uber-taxi-toronto-protest-1.3362193

Iborra, Y.S. (2017) Airbnb pide a sus usuarios que presionen al Ayuntamiento de Barcelona y a la Generalitat contra su regulación [Airbnb asks its users to put pressure on Barcelona Town Hall and the Municipality against regulation]. *eldiario.es*. Available at: https://www.eldiario.es/catalunya/air bnb-presionen-ayuntamiento-barcelona-generalitat_1_3539402.html

IDEA (2024) *Perceptions of Democracy*. International Institute for Democracy and Electoral Assistance Public Report. Available at: https://www.idea. int/sites/default/files/2024-04/perceptions-of-democracy.pdf

Issar, S. and Aneesh, A. (2022) What is algorithmic governance? *Sociology Compass*, 16(1), e12955.

Jad, I. (2004) The NGO-isation of Arab women's movements. *IDS Bulletin*, 35(4), 34–42.

Jolly, J. and Wearden, G. (2024) Landmark moment as Uber unveils first annual profit as limited company. *The Guardian*, 7 February. Available at: https://www.theguardian.com/technology/2024/feb/07/landmark-moment-as-uber-unveils-first-annual-profit-as-limited-company

Juul (2024) *Juul Action Network*. Available at: https://www.juul.com/action network

Kalamar, A. (2013) Sharewashing is the new greenwashing. *OpEdNews.com*, 13 May. Available at: https://www.opednews.com/articles/Sharewashing-is-the-New-Gr-by-Anthony-Kalamar-130513-834.html

Katic, I.V. and Hillman, A. (2023) Corporate political activity, reimagined: revisiting the political marketplace. *Journal of Management*, 49(6), 1911–1938.

Kelly, K. (2016) *The Inevitable: Understanding the 12 Technological Forces that will Shape Our Future*. London: Penguin.

Kostelka, F. and Blais, A. (2021) The generational and institutional sources of the global decline in voter turnout. *World Politics*, 73(4), 629–667.

Koutsimpogiorgos, N., Frenken, K. and Herrmann, A.M. (2023) Platform adaptation to regulation: the case of domestic cleaning in Europe. *Journal of Industrial Relations*, 00221856221146833.

Krugman, P. (2008) *The Return of Depression Economics and the Crisis of 2008*. New York: W.W. Norton and Company.

Lee, D. (2023) Airbnb earnings surge as foreign travel rebounds. *Financial Times*, 14 February. Available at: https://www.ft.com/content/dde65da6-7da2-45fb-935c-c13b339ce45e

Lehdonvirta, V. (2022) *Cloud Empires: How Digital Platforms Are Overtaking the State and How We Can Regain Control*. Cambridge, MA: MIT Press.

Lessig, L. (2011) *Republic, Lost: How Money Corrupts Congress – and a Plan to Stop It*. London: Hachette UK.

Lobbying Transparency (2015) *International Standards for Lobbying Regulation*. Transparency International, Access Info Europe, Sunlight Foundation and Open Knowledge International. Available at: https://lobbyingtransparency.net/

Lynskey, O. (2017) Regulating 'platform power'. London School of Economics Law, Society and Economy Working Papers 1/2017.

Mager, A. and Katzenbach, C. (2021) Future imaginaries in the making and governing of digital technology. *New Media & Society*, 23(2), 223–236. https://doi.org/10.1177/1461444820929321

Manjoo, F. (2018) How tech companies conquered America's cities. *New York Times*, 24 December. Available at: https://nyti.ms/2K26OZO

Marcuse, H. (2002 [1964]) *One-dimensional Man: Studies in the Ideology of Advanced Industrial Society*. Abingdon: Routledge.

Martin, C.J. (2016) The sharing economy: a pathway to sustainability or a nightmarish form of neoliberal capitalism? *Ecological Economics*, 121, 149–159.

Mason, P. (2015) *Postcapitalism: A Guide to Our Future*. London: Penguin.

Mathews, J. (2014) The sharing economy boom is about to bust. *Time Magazine*, 27 June. Available at: https://time.com/2924778/airbnb-uber-sharing-economy/

Mazur, J. and Serafin, M. (2023) Stalling the state: how digital platforms contribute to and profit from delays in the enforcement and adoption of regulations. *Comparative Political Studies*, 56(1), 101–130.

McKinley, J. (2016) Ride-hailing gains prominence for any special session in Albany. *New York Times*, 16 December. Available at: https://www.nytimes.com/2016/12/20/nyregion/ride-hailing-gains-prominence-for-any-special-session-in-albany.html

Melucci, A. (1996) *Challenging Codes: Collective Action in the Information Age*. Cambridge: Cambridge University Press.

Meronek, T. (2014) Tech companies adopt Astroturf to get their (wicked) way. *Truthout*, 20 April. Available at: https://truthout.org/articles/tech-companies-adopt-astroturf-to-get-their-wicked-way/

Meyer, D.S. and Tarrow, S.G. (eds) (1998) *The Social Movement Society: Contentious Politics for a New Century*. Lanham: Rowman & Littlefield.

Micheletti, M. (2003) *Political Virtue and Shopping*. London: Palgrave Macmillan.

Michelon, G., Rodrigue, M. and Trevisan, E. (2020) The marketization of a social movement: activists, shareholders and CSR disclosure. *Accounting, Organizations and Society*, 80, 101074.

Mikołajewska-Zając, K. (2019) The rhetoric of sharing. In R. Belk, G. Eckhardt and F. Bahrdi (eds), *Handbook of the Sharing Economy*. Cheltenham: Edward Elgar, pp 362–374.

Morozov, E. (2013) *To Save Everything, Click Here: The Folly of Technological Solutionism*. London: Allen Lane.

Morozov, E. (2018) From Airbnb to city bikes, the 'sharing economy' has been seized by big money. *The Guardian*, 27 November. Available at: https://www.theguardian.com/commentisfree/2018/nov/27/airbnb-city-bikes-sharing-economy-big-money

Morozov, E. (2022) Critique of techno-feudal reason. *New Left Review*, 133/4, 89–126.

Muldoon, J. (2022) *Platform Socialism*. London: Pluto Press.

Murillo, D., Buckland, H. and Val, E. (2017) When the sharing economy becomes neoliberalism on steroids. *Technological Forecasting and Social Change*, 125, 66–76.

Murphy, C. (2020) Uber bought itself a law. *The Guardian*, 12 November. Available at: https://www.theguardian.com/commentisfree/2020/nov/12/uber-prop-22-law-drivers-ab5-gig-workers

Nestle, M. (2019) *Food Politics: How the Food Industry Influences Nutrition and Health*. Oakland, CA: University of California Press.

Nieborg, D.B. and Poell, T. (2018) The platformization of cultural production: theorizing the contingent cultural commodity. *New Media & Society*, 20(11), 4275–4292.

Nieuwland, S. and van Melik, R. (2020) Regulating Airbnb. *Current Issues in Tourism*, 23(7), 811–825. https://doi.org/10.1080/13683 500.2018.1504899

Novy, J. and Colomb, C. (2019) Urban tourism as a source of contention and social mobilisations: a critical review. *Tourism Planning and Development*, 16(4), 358–375. https://doi.org/10.1080/21568316.2019.1577293

Nyberg, D. and Murray, J. (2023) Corporate populism: how corporations construct and represent 'the people' in political contestations. *Journal of Business Research*, 162. https://doi.org/10.1016/j.jbusres.2023.113879

Occhiuto, N. (2021) Enabling disruptive innovations: a comparative case study of Uber in New York City, Chicago and San Francisco. *Socio-Economic Review*, 20(4), 1881–1903.

OED (2024) Independence. Available at: https://www.oed.com/search/dic tionary/?scope=Entries&q=independence

Oppegaard, S.M., Saari, T. and Saloniemi, A. (2020) Uber's trajectories in the Nordic countries. In K. Jesnes and S.M. Nordli Oppegaard (eds), *Platform Work in the Nordic Models, TemaNord Report*, 513. Available at: https://pub.norden.org/temanord2020-513/

Polanyi, K. (2001) *The Great Transformation: The Political and Economic Origins of Our Time*, 2nd edn. Boston: Beacon Press.

Polletta, F. (2008) Storytelling in politics. *Contexts*, 7(4), 26–31.

Pollman, E. and Barry, J.M. (2016) Regulatory entrepreneurship. *Southern Californian Law Review*, 90, 383–448.

PRC (2015) *The 13th Five-Year Plan for Economic and Social Development of the People's Republic of China*. Available at: https://en.ndrc.gov.cn/policies/202105/P020210527785800103339.pdf

Putnam, R.D. (2000) *Bowling Alone: The Collapse and Revival of American Community*. London: Simon & Schuster.

Ravenelle, A.J. (2019) *Hustle and Gig: Struggling and Surviving in the Sharing Economy*. Oakland: University of California Press.

Rhodes, C. (2021) *Woke Capitalism: How Corporate Morality is Sabotaging Democracy*. Bristol: Policy Press.

Rosenblat, A. (2018) *Uberland: How Algorithms are Rewriting the Rules of Work*. Berkeley: University of California Press.

Rosenblat, A. (2019) Uber and the doublespeak at the heart of Silicon Valley. *Fast Company*, 5 October. Available at: https://www.fastcompany.com/90347393/uber-and-the-doublespeak-at-the-heart-of-silicon-valley

Rosenblat, A. and Stark, L. (2016) Algorithmic labor and information asymmetries: a case study of Uber's drivers. *International Journal of Communication*, 10, 27.

Santos, B.S. (2004) The World Social Forum: toward a counter-hegemonic globalization. In P. Sen, J. Anand, A. Escobar and A. Waterman (eds), *The World Social Forum: Challenging Empires*. New Delhi: The Viveka Foundation, pp 235–245.

Scholz, T. (2017) *Uberworked and Underpaid: How Workers are Disrupting the Digital Economy*. Hoboken: John Wiley & Sons.

Scholz, T. and Schneider, N. (2017) *Ours to Hack and to Own: The Rise of Platform Cooperativism, a New Vision for the Future of Work and a Fairer Internet*. New York: OR Books.

Schor, J.B. (2007) In defense of consumer critique. *The Annals of the American Academy of Political and Social Science*, 611(1), 16–30.

Schor, J. (2016) Debating the sharing economy. *Journal of Self-governance and Management Economics*, 4(3), 7–22.

Schor, J.B. and Attwood-Charles, W. (2017) The 'sharing' economy: labor, inequality, and social connection on for-profit platforms. *Sociology Compass*, 11(8), e12493.

Schor, J.B. and Vallas, S.P. (2021) The sharing economy: rhetoric and reality. *Annual Review of Sociology*, 47, 369–389.

Schüßler, E., Attwood-Charles, W., Kirchner, S. and Schor, J.B. (2021) Between mutuality, autonomy and domination. *Socio-Economic Review*, 19(4), 1217–1243.

Seidl, T. (2022) The politics of platform capitalism: a case study on the regulation of Uber in New York. *Regulation & Governance*, 16(2), 357–374.

Serafin, M. (2019) Contesting the digital economy: struggles over Uber in Poland. In S. Schiller-Merkens and P. Balsiger (eds), *The Contested Moralities of Markets*. Leeds: Emerald Publishing Limited, pp 187–201.

Shiltagh, M. (2024) Deliveroo posts first-ever profit, sees further improvements. *Bloomberg*, 13 March. Available at: https://www.bloomb erg.com/news/articles/2024-03-14/deliveroo-posts-first-ever-profit-sees-further-improvements

Slee, T. (2015) *What's Yours is Mine: Against the Sharing Economy*. New York: OR Books.

Soper, K. and Trentmann, F. (eds) (2008) *Citizenship and Consumption*. Basingstoke and New York: Palgrave Macmillan.

Soriano, C.R. (2023) Solidarity and resistance meet social enterprise: the social logic of alternative cloudwork platforms. *International Journal of Communication*, 17. Available at: https://ijoc.org/index.php/ijoc/article/view/17762

Srnicek, N. (2016) *Platform Capitalism*. Cambridge: Polity.

Stabrowski, F. (2017) 'People as businesses': Airbnb and urban micro-entrepreneurialism in New York City. *Cambridge Journal of Regions, Economy and Society*, 10(2), 327–347.

Stabrowski, F. (2022) Political organizing and narrative framing in the sharing economy. *City*, 26(1), 142–159.

Staley, O. (2017) Uber has replaced Travis Kalanick's values with eight new 'cultural norms'. *Quartz*, 7 November. Available at: https://qz.com/work/1123038/uber-has-replaced-travis-kalanicks-values-with-eight-new-cultural-normsTropes

Standing on Giants (2023) Airbnb: Building a global community of hosts. Available at: https://www.standingongiants.com/case-studies/airbnb-building-a-global-community-of-hosts/

Statista (2024) Total lobbying spending in the United States from 1998 to 2023. Available at: https://www.statista.com/statistics/257337/total-lobby ing-spending-in-the-us/

Stehlin, J. and Payne, W. (2023) Disposable infrastructures: 'micromobility' platforms and the political economy of transport disruption in Austin, Texas. *Urban Studies*, 60(2), 274–291.

Stiglitz, J. (2010) *Freefall: Free Markets and the Sinking of the Global Economy*. London: Penguin.

Stole, I.L. (2008) Philanthropy as public relations: a critical perspective on cause marketing. *International Journal of Communication*, 2, 20–40.

Strauss, A.L. and Corbin, J. (1998) *Basics of Qualitative Research: Techniques and Procedures for Developing Grounded Theory*. Thousand Oaks: SAGE.

Streeck, W. (2012) Considerations on the new politics of consumption. *New Left Review*, 76, 27–47.

Sundararajan, A. (2016) *The Sharing Economy: The End of Employment and the Rise of Crowd-based Capitalism*. Cambridge, MA: MIT Press.

Tassinari, A. and Maccarrone, V. (2020) Riders on the storm: workplace solidarity among gig economy couriers in Italy and the UK. *Work, Employment and Society*, 34(1), 35–54.

Thelen, K. (2018) Regulating Uber. *Perspectives on Politics*, 16(4), 938–953.

Thoreau, H.D. (1993) *Civil Disobedience and Other Essays*. New York: Dover.

Ticona, J. (2022) Red flags, sob stories, and scams: the contested meaning of governance on carework labor platforms. *New Media & Society*, 24(7), 1548–1566.

Ticona, J., Mateescu, A. and Rosenblat, A. (2018) Beyond disruption: how tech shapes labor across domestic work and ridehailing. *Data & Society*, 27 June. Available at: https://datasociety.net/output/beyond-disruption/

Tilly, C. (2004) *Social Movements, 1768–2004*. Boulder: Paradigm Publishers.

Tinsley, M. (2021) *Commemorating Muslims in the First World War Centenary: Making Melancholia*. London: Routledge.

Tobacco Tactics (2022) Industry tactics. Available at: https://tobaccotactics.org/topics/industry-tactics/

Tomassetti, J. (2016) Does Uber redefine the firm: the postindustrial corporation and advanced information technology. *Hofstra Labor & Employment Law Journal*, 34(1), Article 3.

Törnberg, P. (2023) How platforms govern: social regulation in digital capitalism. *Big Data & Society*, 10(1), 20539517231153808.

Transparency International (2015) *Lobbying in Europe*. Available at: https://www.transparency.org/en/publications/lobbying-in-europe

Transparency International Ireland (2015) *Responsible Lobbying: A Short Guide to Ethical Lobbying and Public Policy Engagement for Professionals, Executives and Activists*. Available at: https://transparency.ie/resources/lobbying/responsible-lobbying

Trentmann, F. (2007) Citizenship and consumption. *Journal of Consumer Culture*, 7(2), 147–158.

Tzur, A. (2019) Uber Über regulation? Regulatory change following the emergence of new technologies in the taxi market. *Regulation & Governance*, 13(3), 340–361.

Uber London (2017) Save your Uber in London. Public petition, Change. org. Available at: https://www.change.org/p/save-your-uber-in-london-saveyouruber

UGT (2021) *Análisis de la presión política y social de las plataformas de reparto* [Analysis of the social and political pressure of sharing economy platforms]. Available at: https://www.ugt.es/sites/default/files/analisis_presion_politica_social_plataformas_reparto-informe.pdf

Uzunca, B., Rigtering, J.C. and Ozcan, P. (2018) Sharing and shaping: a cross-country comparison of how sharing economy firms shape their institutional environment to gain legitimacy. *Academy of Management Discoveries*, 4(3), 248–272.

Valdez, J. (2023) The politics of Uber: infrastructural power in the United States and Europe. *Regulation & Governance*, 17(1), 177–194.

Van Deth, J.W. (2001) Studying political participation: towards a theory of everything. *Joint Sessions of Workshops of the European Consortium for Political Research*, April. Grenoble.

Van Dijck, J., Poell, T. and De Waal, M. (2018) *The Platform Society: Public Values in a Connective World*. Oxford: Oxford University Press.

Van Doorn, N. (2020) A new institution on the block. *New Media and Society*, 22(10), 1808–1826.

Varoufakis, Y. (2023) *Technofeudalism: What Killed Capitalism*. London: Vintage.

Vedantam, K. (2019) Airbnb, NAACP partner to get more people of color to become Airbnb hosts. *The Spokesman Review*, 9 June. Available at: https://www.spokesman.com/stories/2019/jun/09/airbnb-naacp-partner-to-get-more-people-of-color-t/

Vrikki, P. and Lekakis, E. (2023) Digital consumers and platform workers unite and fight? The platformisation of consumer activism in the case of #cancel_efood in Greece. *Marketing Theory*, 14705931231195191.

Wachsmuth, D. and Weisler, A. (2018) Airbnb and the rent gap. *Environment and Planning A*, 50(6), 1147–1170.

Walker, E.T. (2014) *Grassroots for Hire*. Cambridge: Cambridge University Press.

Walker, E.T. and Rea, C.M. (2014) The political mobilization of firms and industries. *Annual Review of Sociology*, 40, 281–304.

Waterhouse, B.C. (2013) *Lobbying America*. Princeton: Princeton University Press.

Waters, R. (2023) Uber makes first operating profit after racking up $31.5bn of losses. *Financial Times*, 1 August. Available at: https://www.ft.com/content/dae2b90e-1ba0-4e8f-aabc-34aae4ca05d7

Wellhausen, R.L. (2016) Recent trends in investor–state dispute settlement. *Journal of International Dispute Settlement*, 7(1), 117–135.

Wilk, R. (2001) Consuming morality. *Journal of Consumer Culture*, 1(2), 245–260.

Wilson, J., Garay-Tamajon, L. and Morales-Perez, S. (2022) Politicising platform-mediated tourism rentals in the digital sphere: Airbnb in Madrid and Barcelona. *Journal of Sustainable Tourism*, 30(5), 1080–1101. https://doi.org/10.1080/09669582.2020.1866585

Wolin, S.S. (2017) *Democracy Incorporated: Managed Democracy and the Specter of Inverted Totalitarianism*. Princeton: Princeton University Press.

Wood, A.J. and Lehdonvirta, V. (2021) Antagonism beyond employment: how the 'subordinated agency' of labour platforms generates conflict in the remote gig economy. *Socio-Economic Review*, 19(4), 1369–1396. https://doi.org/10.1093/ser/mwab016

Woodcock, J. (2021) *The Fight against Platform Capitalism: An Inquiry into the Global Struggles of the Gig Economy*. London: University of Westminster Press.

Woodcock, J. and Cant, C. (2022) Platform worker organising at Deliveroo in the UK. *Journal of Labor and Society*, 25(2), 220–236. https://doi.org/10.1163/24714607-bja10050

Wright, E.O. (2010) *Envisioning Real Utopias*. London: Verso.

Yates, L. (2018) Sharing, households and sustainable consumption. *Journal of Consumer Culture*, 18(3), 433–452.

Yates, L. (2020) The politics of the platform economy. In M. Hodson, J. Kasmire, A. McMeekin, J.G. Stehlin and K. Ward (eds), *Urban Platforms and the Future City*. London: Routledge, pp 120–133.

Yates, L. (2021) The Airbnb 'movement' for deregulation: how platform-sponsored grassroots lobbying is changing politics. *Ethical Consumer*. Available at: https://research.ethicalconsumer.org/research-hub/ethical-consumption-review/airbnbs-growing-political-power

Yates, L. (2023) How platform businesses mobilize their users and allies: corporate grassroots lobbying and the Airbnb 'movement' for deregulation. *Socio-Economic Review*, 21(4), 1917–1943.

Yates, L., Daniel, A., Gerharz, E. and Feldman, S. (2024) Foregrounding social movement futures: collective action, imagination, and methodology. *Social Movement Studies*, 23(4), 429–445.

Yin, R. (2011) *Applications of Case Study Research*. Thousand Oaks: SAGE.

Zuboff, S. (2019) *The Age of Surveillance Capitalism*. London: Profile Books.

Index

References to figures appear in *italic* type; those in **bold** type refer to tables.
References to endnotes show both the page number and the note number (110n1).